PRAISE FOR FLYING IN THE FACE OF GRIEF

This book holds the keys to activate our deeper awareness of eternal life. Through the author's journey we see how the loss of a loved one opens the potential for us to find the deep love for ourself. She leaves no doubt that grief is our greatest guide into the heart of our truth. ANNWYN has clearly mapped the way for us all, in sharing herself so intimately within this powerfully, beautiful book. I loved every word.

Janine Savient, 'The Heart Lady'

An extraordinary story of one person's transformation of grief; not just any person, this is ANNWYN, a way shower. Her story is infused with energetic codes that will provide a paradigm shift for the reader, and usher in new understanding for those who deeply grieve the loss of loved ones.

Karen Bowller
Light Activator of the Heart.

This book offers a chrysalis-like safe space that allows the start of a miraculous transformation. As a mother myself who recently lost her beloved son, this book soothed me like gifted fingers gently plucking taut guitar strings. An ethereal melody resonated in my heart, silencing the self-doubt of my own heavenly experiences and encouraging me to trust in the knowing that 'no one ever really dies'. Annwyn's personal account is written with a sensitive, honest and brave heart. Her pin-pointing metaphors express a myriad of emotions that describe her personal experiences. For those who dare to 'fly in the face of grief' an invitation is offered to explore the transformational dimension that is fuelled by love, not fear. I have discovered that 'the way' we grieve can become an inspiring journey.

Claudia W.
BSC, MA Linguistics, Art Therapist,
Reiki Practitioner

This uplifting and beautifully written book takes readers to new dimensions of understanding life's journey. ANNWYN offers deep and illuminating insights into the rich worlds of the emotional and spiritual terrain of loss. Not only providing a roadmap through grief but transcending it into emotional mastery. It is a deeply reflective and healing read.

Terri Morehu
Author of 'The Only Way Out Is In.'

I read this beautiful book to my eleven-year-old daughter, Phoebe, and from start to finish, we went through Annette's journey together. The first chapter was fraught for both of us with the story of Tim's sudden death, but when Annette had to tell her daughter while knowing it could destroy her life, we were both in tears. Phoebe loved the funeral chapter and wanted to be there, along with all of Tim's friends to add her magic touch painting the coffin. As we progressed through Annette's experiences, we talked about people dying and the effect it had on all those close to them. And we both saw how Annette responded each time to poignant moments of choice, cheering her on each time she unreservedly said, 'Yes to life!' We saw how the piercing of her Heart, launched her into the quest of a lifetime, a quest to find out 'why?'

and 'what's it all about?' It was a quest for perspective, to see beyond the apparent. And Annette could only climb the mast to get a bigger picture by allowing herself to change, hoisting up the skirts of her identity as she went, shrugging off her assumed 'Corky' identity and releasing all she had ever thought she was.

Phoebe's response to the book was "I think people will find this very helpful when somebody dies."

I love the guiding principle which at every choice-point opened her to inner change and necessary healing of her Heart, giving her freedom and experiences otherwise not possible. ANNWYN is a trail blazer. This book will help readers to see grief as an opportunity, not a burden.

Raeul Pierard
MMus, New Zealand Cellist

ANNWYN says she wants to 'soften the journey of transformation'. She has achieved this. Sharing an offering of inspired beauty, release and freedom she describes profoundly the possibilities of the grief process and offers sage lessons.

A deep understanding of the magic in the power we call the grief experience is evident. She opens the reality of connection and of seership, satisfying not needing to be 'boxed in' by our tendency to support an existing paradigm. Tim's words and messages are treasures!

I felt a mutual caring warm embrace throughout ANNWYN'S raw self-reflection. Her interspersed insight, honesty, adventure and humour is delightful. I laughed, cried, my heart swelled. I recognised sadness with a deeper joy.

Kirsty Morton
–Theosophical Society NZ chairperson.

FLYING IN THE FACE OF GRIEF

The Ever Being of Life

"Death is a stripping away of all that is not you.
The secret of life is to 'die before you die' - and find that there is
no death."

Eckhart Tolle

ANNWYN

Katoosh Publishing NZ
New Zealand 2025

Copyright © Katoosh Publishing NZ 2025
All rights reserved.
No part of this book may be reproduced in any form or by any electronic or mechanical means, including information storage, and retrieval systems, without written permission from the publisher, except for the use of brief quotations in a book review.

Flying in the Face of Grief, first published in 2025
A catalogue record of this book is held at the National Library of New Zealand

ISBN 978-0-473-72707-9 Paperback
ISBN 978-0-473-72708-6 Epub
Cover design: Melli M Designs
Book Interior and E-book formatting by
Amit Dey (amitdey2528@gmail.com)

First version published as 'Dry Your Tears'
Little Grace Publishing, New Zealand, 2012

Katoosh Publishing NZ
Please contact ANNWYN
www.annwynvibe.com
annwynvibe@gmail.com
+64 (0) 21 0295 9233
New Zealand

For anyone who has ever wondered about the higher purpose of grief. Also, what happens during transition to the afterlife and, the continuity of life.

TABLE OF CONTENTS

Introduction xi
1. Sound of a Breaking Heart 1
2. Otherworldly Owl 13
3. Life Continues for All 27
4. Bright Soul 39
5. Pantry of Love and Pain 53
6. Soul Dilemma 63
7. Dream Pockets 75
8. Soul and Ship Mates 93
9. Rocking the Boat 109
10. Surrender 121
11. Dark Night of the Soul 133
12. Babushka Doll 139
13. Soul Lessons 151
14. New Path 157
15. Soul Key 171
16. Heart of Gaia 185
17. City of Light 197
18. Sacred Closure 211
19. Dropping Out 217
20. Spirit and Heart Wisdom 219
21. My Ever Being Life 241
Epilogue 253
About ANNWYN 257
Acknowledgements 259

INTRODUCTION

"*W*here are you my darling boy … did you suffer?" I was desperate to know. My arms wound tightly around Laura's small frame, my chest heaving against hers. She screamed out in pain, accusing her seventeen-year-old brother, "You left me!"

It soon became clear I couldn't settle for the well-intentioned expectations of others - that 'I'd never recover from Tim's death.' At least, not after hearing curious murmurings within hours of his car crash, "Remember, remember - it's time to remember now." A sweet, otherworldly cloak of love enshrouded me for weeks, coaxing me with whispered prompts to remember.

But remember what - and why now of all times?

An unexpected pilgrimage began. Over the ensuing months and years, a rite of passage revealed itself - one we have mistakenly called 'crippling grief'. Mostly, the noble gifts of grief have lain crumpled on the floor, creased with sorrow, unrecognised.

At times these gifts brought me to my knees but, finally, I understood 'the hero's journey' where wants and needs must eventually collide in unlit corridors called the dark night of the soul. I ached to commune with my son, and I desired to know about the afterlife. More than that, I urgently needed to find my own purpose for being on Earth at all, because up until that point I had lived my life through others. But to achieve this I would have to identify and release my erroneous beliefs about death and grief, along with a quantum shift in my consciousness. Only then would the healing of my heart occur, opening the portal where physical and nonphysical worlds could meet.

> *There is soul's purpose in grieving,*
> *for we have not lost our loved ones,*
> *we have lost ourselves.*
> *Our beloved departed souls will lovingly guide*
> *us back - if we allow them.*
> *Remember?*

When Tim transitioned back into Spirit in 2000, I yearned for the information held within these pages. I needed to hear from others who had experienced grief and, while professionals held their important, rightful place, I intuitively bypassed conventional models of therapy offered at that time. I scoured the piles of books next to my bed, each time dissatisfied with the answers; there had to be more!

Grief had reached into every little pocket of my human nature - it's no wonder at first I avoided it like the plague. Besides, I wanted to know why I didn't believe this was the end of Tim's life. Hearing about soul contracts and soul lessons, ascended masters, I became fascinated by the concept of my own my higher self.

It wasn't until I began writing that I realised I'd organically embodied the structure of universal story accredited to Joseph Campbell as the 'hero's journey'. I realised too that all

INTRODUCTION

of humanity are unsung heroes, bravely meshing their wants and needs while undergoing the changes that transform them into better versions.

I have republished this extensively revised and updated version because, although the world and humanity are much changed, death remains one of humanity's deepest fears. Grief is still perceived as an undesired burden, instead of a richly transformative opportunity. And, there really is more, because around the same time that I fully understood there was no death, Tim announced he had joined a collective of souls known as 'Katoosh'. The meaning of that name is 'universal-eternal-love.'

Eckhart Tolle once wrote, 'we don't need to sit on a park bench for two years,' as he did after experiencing suicidal thoughts, and neither do we need to avoid grief by 'running away to sea' and cruising the Pacific Islands for six years as I did. Tolle's books were pivotal for me; he flew in the face of what humanity believed to be 'normal' human nature. In the same spirit of Eckhart's messages, I wish to soften and even shorten the journey of transformation, because the last leg of the hero's journey involves sharing wisdom gained.

Soar with me beneath the wings of ascended masters and my son in spirit. Liberate yourself from acquired beliefs regarding life and death. Discover an inner sanctum of wisdom where death no longer dwells, only the ever-being-of-life.

Together, we will fly in the face of grief!

Chapter 1

SOUND OF A BREAKING HEART

*'In this curious, calm state of grace,
something mysterious stirred within me.'*

Tim has churned with agitation for days, a six-foot tall jangle of teenage nerves. No amount of coaxing can persuade him to confide. At last, choking back emotions, he opens up.

Tears wet his sun-kissed freckles as he splutters, "I can't stop thinking about Floyd and Jess. I can't get them out of my mind, Mumsy. It's like they're living in my head. At night, they call me. I can't sleep."

Three months earlier, both teenagers had taken their lives within weeks of each other. While the rest of the world lost sleep over technology crashing from the millennium bug, a spate of teenage suicides rocked our small harbourside town of Lyttelton, New Zealand.

FLYING IN THE FACE OF GRIEF — BY ANNWYN

Allowing me to fuss, I plump cushions and soft rugs around him on the sofa. Taking a damp flannel to cool his forehead, I stroke the worry from his surf-bleached curls. A rock fan at heart, he surrenders to soothing classical music and soon dozes off. He looks so peaceful sleeping away the winter evening.

I gaze down at my golden boy, admiring his youthful beauty. His long legs dangle over the end of the sofa, auburn hairs showing beneath scrunched up trousers. Fast morphing into manhood, Tim loves fashionable clothes and I smile at how he's managed to make navy work-overalls look trendy.

Sighing as the kettle warmed, I thought back to the past nightmarish nine months. At times, Tim's recovery from a drug-induced psychotic episode had relapsed into serious unwellness. For many months I lived with the prospect he might take his own life but, thank God, step by step he had stabilised. Supported by his understanding boss, Tim now held down a job as a hammer hand at the new Lyttelton marina, but a sensitive young man such as he would of course feel the impact of not just one, but two suicides. I hoped like hell his healing would continue.

An hour or so later he wakes and sits bolt upright.

"How are you feeling, love?"

"Better, Mumsy. I dreamed of an amazing wave. I'm going to draw it."

Drawers open and close, and clothes fly through the air before a packet of coloured pencils turns up. I'm reassured by his complete focus sketching a surfer riding a perfect tube and, it's difficult to believe an hour earlier this young man struggled to finish a sentence. Not only has he now captured the wave with his natural artistic ability, but the dream also seems to have harnessed the peace he yearns for.

"Looks like your favourite break. Sumner Beach?"

"Not sure what beach this is. It seemed so real in my dream. I could even taste the salt. Thanks, Mumsy, I think I'll be able to sleep tonight."

I love the way he calls me Mumsy, a Tim thing. Resting my face against his chest for a moment I feel the strength in his body. After giving me a lopsided grin and a bear hug, he ambles off to his new double bed, purchased with his first pay packet.

Waking next morning with a cough rattling in his chest, Tim decides to take the day off work to see his doctor. I long to stay home with him, but he insists I go. I remain unconvinced, but with my car undergoing major mechanical repair, a forthcoming bill overrides my maternal misgivings. Hearing the chuff and hum of a colleague's Volkswagen Beetle arriving to give me a lift, I promise to ring during my lunch break and head out the door.

With the ease of a seasoned actress, I swing into my role as the cheerful, resilient, single parent who teaches school 'dropouts' to decode the inky symbols on their pages. Parenting my own teenagers, plus specialised training for dyslexic students has prepared me well for this position. It makes me mindful of the enormous pressures young people are under, and that my students' apparent failure adds to their vulnerability. They are unaware the system has failed them - not the other way around.

Teaching duties command my full attention until lunch break allows me to phone Tim. Sounding confident and upbeat he says, "Doc prescribed antibiotics for a chest infection. I've cleaned up my room."

"Wow! You must be really feeling unwell." I shake my head in disbelief.

"Very funny, Mumsy. I'm going over to Sumner to visit Dad. See you tonight."

On a more serious note, I say, "Take it easy, darling. A chest infection means your body needs rest."

"Don't worry Mumsy, I'm fine. Love you."

"Love you too," I echo. My steps and thoughts are lighter heading back to the staffroom. He's just a little run down. Things feel worse when under the weather. His voice sounded cheerful. Thank heavens.

Tim isn't home at the end of the day. I expected to find him curled up watching a movie or listening to music. The phone rings the moment I fling my battered teaching folders onto a chair. It's Elaine, a friend who purchased our former family home a few weeks ago.

"Annette, thank God. I've been trying to get hold of you all afternoon," she says in a rushed, breathless voice. "Two detectives were looking for you earlier. I gave them your new address. They want you to ring Lyttelton police station straight away."

A multitude of scenarios rush through my mind as I dial the station's number. Staff straight away dispatch the two detectives who have waited hours for my call.

Telling myself to remain calm, I reason there is nothing much I can't handle. After two completed marriages and raising teenagers alone it takes a fair bit to phase me. Both children are high-spirited individuals, especially Laura who's known among friends with affection as the 'wild child'. Tim practices discretion, whereas Laura tends to be impulsive.

Impulsive to such a degree I've sent her to live with friends in the remote alpine village of Mount Cook.

Her substitute 'mother' is the sole teacher at the local tiny school, and I remember she's running their annual school camp in Hanmer Springs. Jumping at the chance to join the ten children she adores, Laura had volunteered to assist. I'd be surprised if she created havoc there. Perhaps she is injured? Assuming Tim is dining with his father, I'm baffled.

I hear the gravel scrunch under the wheels of the police car in the car park. Hurried steps ascend the wooden stairway and urgent knuckles rap on my door. Forcing a warm greeting, I invite the two tall strangers to sit but they remain standing. A palpable tension, like over-tightened guitar strings, exudes from these men in my living room. After the formality of checking I am indeed Annette Hanham, they introduce themselves, encouraging me to sit down. I stand. Taller feels stronger, braver. I brace myself, clenching my buttocks.

One of the detectives again advises me to be seated, indicating a chair and warning they bring bad news.

"How bad?" I ask, my heart thumping.

"Your son has been in a car accident."

Blood drains from my face, my mouth all at once dry. "How bad?"

"The worst," they say. Then silence, as they allow me time to prepare for words no mother wants to hear.

"Do you mean ... (silence) ... he's ... dead?"

"Yes. We can't tell you how sorry we are to bring you this news."

My tall tower of bravery collapses and topples me into the nearest chair. Hot drops of salt sting my eyes and surge down my cheeks. Blinded and doubled over with shock, I sob out loud, hands over my face in primal privacy. My heart rips, like the tearing during a birthing. Pain sears my chest, but there is no midwife to hold me. It's violent; I think my ribs will crack. Remembering the detectives are still there and, feeling genuine pity for their difficult task I manage to look up and sob, "What an awful job you have."

A mix of relief and gratitude passes over their faces and, they take their cue to tell me what happened. "Your son was travelling along Sumner Road, between Lyttelton and Sumner on a patch where heavy rain had brought minerals up to the surface. On top of this, a tanker from Lyttelton Port leaked a trail of oil on that road earlier today. We are trying to find the driver responsible."

The second detective takes over and speaks with a modicum of warmth in his voice. "However, we think Tim may have been driving a little too fast. When he braked at a tight corner, his car spun around on the greasy road. The car slid into the cliff face hitting an overhanging rock. We believe he died straight away on impact, around 1.30pm."

Weeping in the chair, I'm in desperate need of strong comforting arms, but the men shift their weight, looking uncomfortable and helpless. All they can offer is professional kindness. One softens his tone, asking if he can phone someone for me.

Friends come straight away, their faces showing deep shock. Older than me and wiser about life, they hold me tight in their ample arms. My thoughts are already a two-hour drive away, with Laura. Thank God it isn't five hours to Mount Cook. Tangled knots pull even tighter in my stomach as I fret. How can I tell her? How can I deliver total devastation?

This familiar dread. The same feeling a year ago, after admitting Tim to the mental hospital then dragging myself away. To have walked away from him in such a vulnerable state had torn me to pieces. I thought I'd faced the most heartbreaking moment in my life but now, even that paled in comparison.

An emotional heaviness crushes my chest, knocking the wind out of me. Before I can draw breath the detectives pass their temporary burden to me like a baton. In this split second I am forced to accept responsibility for this permanent change to our lives. Worst of all, the baton of bad news must be taken to Laura.

I ring Johnny, Tim's boss. Because Johnny understood the nature of Tim's condition, he'd kept a lookout for Tim, and we'd become friends. Stunned by my news, he offers to drive me to Laura. He arrives ashen-faced and together we collect my close friend, April.

The night drive is a blur, almost surreal. I don't feel like talking. I'm crying at times, but my focus is on holding myself together for Laura.

April is inconsolable. "I feel like I've lost a son too," she wails.

"Remember our little boys holding hands and walking to school together?" I say, squeezing her hand.

"Yes, Timmy and Jimmy." She nods, "And years later they started work at the marina on the same day."

"Tim said it was awesome to see a familiar face. But just a handshake that time," I say with an unsuccessful attempt to lighten the mood.

"God, I'm supposed be supporting you. I'm sorry, I can't stop crying."

"Johnny," I say, leaning forward to be heard over the road noise, "better stop at a shop for a box of tissues."

Putting my arm around my friend, "I think when one parent loses a child, every parent loses a child. There's an unspoken bond among the parents whose children grow up together."

Then, losing myself in nightmarish thoughts, I question how it was possible to have been teaching remedial maths earlier today, unaware that firefighters were cutting my son from a wreckage.

Was I that disconnected from my son?

Where was my mother's instinct?

How could I not have felt that?

Remorse finds a dark crevice in my belly and crawls in to feast. Oh, how I wish I had stayed home today. Now, the headlights light up the road signs, announcing we are getting closer to the school camp, closer to Laura. My hunched body aches with dread. I rub my sweaty palms slowly up and down my knees, aware of a high-pitched static noise in my ears.

Tim and Laura are devoted siblings. Twenty-two months apart, they idolise and support each other through the unhappy times as well as the crazy, joyful times of life. Laura looks up to her brother with adoration, manages his hair and wardrobe, shares his secrets, and screens all his girlfriends.

Tim (15) and Laura (13), devoted siblings.

It's been a year since she had made the world-famous, yet isolated village of Mount Cook (Aoraki) her home with close family friends, Brian and Bu. We all agreed Laura needed a break from Lyttelton after abrupt, marked changes in her behaviour caused serious concern for her safety. Her changed environment had proved an astounding success, and the Hermitage Hotel were quick to recognise Laura's natural hospitality skills. They thought her older than her years but, still hired her on condition she continued living with Bu and Brian rather than in staff quarters. Laura and Tim had never lived apart for any length of time before and, although they missed each other, both had recognised the need.

We are now just ten minutes from Hanmer Springs; I ask Johnny to stop the car. I stumble out with unsteady legs and pace around in circles. Panic sets in, I feel sick. There's a band tight around my chest leaving me breathless.

Desperate to steady myself, my mind makes a frantic search for words to lessen the impact. There are no right words - what words could even come close to softening this devastating blow? To spare Laura an anxious long wait, I hold back my arrival as long as possible, but as we approach the gates to the camping ground, I must now phone Bu. Alarmed by my call, she warns Laura I'm here, and to prepare for bad news.

It's close to 9pm. Through the hut window I see the small group of children and parent helpers sitting in the camp kitchen clutching steaming mugs of drinks. Laura appears at the open doorway, her long, blonde hair held back by a blue paisley bandana. She looks worried and pale. Bu takes her arm and guides her out into the crisp dark night, leaving the concerned, cocoa-smeared faces of the children in the warm glow of the kitchen.

FLYING IN THE FACE OF GRIEF — BY ANNWYN

This close, I see her large dark brown eyes are wide with adrenaline and filled with worry. We have never looked at each other in this way before: pleading in her eyes, anguish in mine.

I try in vain to muster strength and courage, but find I can't speak, can't breathe. Paralysed with fear of what these words will do to her, my mouth understands my dilemma - it opens and closes, but nothing comes.

April steps forward, bravely offering to be my voice in this dreadful moment, but I shake my head. It's my responsibility to speak the unspeakable. There is no saliva in my mouth and as I falter again, Bu takes charge in true matriarchal style and commands, "Out with it!"

It seems as if someone else's voice utters the words that I'm so reluctant to ground in reality, but I hear myself say, "It's Tim, there's been an accident."

Laura freezes. Horror steals over her beautiful face as she realises the nature of my words. "No, she says, he's not ...?"

"Yes," is all I can whisper. I hang my head and watch large drops of water fall on the small, smooth stones.

Laura's scream shatters the peaceful alpine air. Like panes of ice. I hear the cracking of her heart as it splinters into tiny, sharp shards of pain. She screams out to her brother, a wild mountain-cat shrieking into the abyss, "Tim! You left me!"

Six strong arms attempt to hold her as she thrashes about in disbelief. She turns wild, flinging her arms to slough off words she can't bear to have near her. Her personal universe implodes in just one second. Eight arms wrestle, like an alpine octopus of angst.

Frozen fingers tear at my womb as I watch my sobbing daughter writhe in agony, resolute in her refusal to know what she now knows. Registering a second death that day, I witness a part of her wither and die. Submerged in a swamp of shocking inadequacy I slump to my knees, realising nothing can ease her pain.

She begins to shake. April wraps her in blankets and bundles her into the back seat of Johnny's car. She whimpers with emotional exhaustion that sweeps her close to physical collapse. With her head resting on my lap, she lays down her distress and succumbs to the void of sleep.

I fall silent during the drive back to the house. It's odd, but now I don't feel disturbed. The day's events no longer run through my head. But I notice a peculiar tingling sensation in my crown. I'm dimly aware of 'something else' surrounding me, embracing me. I, too, am wrapped in a blanket, but mine is invisible. A soothing cocoon crafted by an unseen force, whose deft fingers weave calm and quietude. My mind can't understand or analyse this strange state. It simply observes.

In this curious, calm state of grace, something mysterious stirs within me, something I've never noticed before. I don't know what this new state is, but I feel reassurance and deep gratitude for this unexpected exodus of acute grief.

Johnny helps us stumble up the stairs, then leaves us by ourselves. The apartment seems much larger than it used to be. Tim will never fill it again.

We sleep in his double bed that night, comforted by his linen library of familiar smells, aftershave and hair mousse. But the earlier acceptance and allowance that held me, has withdrawn its embrace. My heart and mind fill with fresh anxiety. Laura and I hug each other and wonder where Tim is, worrying he suffered at his death. Numb with exhaustion, we cry ourselves to sleep. Laura sobs for her brother. I wail for both my children, and my womb bleeds sticky tears between my legs.

Chapter 2

OTHERWORLDLY OWL

*'I watched Tim shape-shift
into a magnificent white owl.
He raised and lowered wondrous wings,
before spreading his feathers
to fly upwards and away.'*

*F*orgetting life has changed, I leisurely stretch out my limbs with a sense of luxury and lazily rub the lids of my eyes. They feel unusually heavy from an exodus of long, deep sleep. Until a jab of memory yanks back the night-time veil; I turn to look at Laura and burst into tears. The first morning of our new life comes all too soon. How I long to sleep again.

"Mum, as soon as Bu said you were on your way to see me ... I knew." Dragging a sleeve across her eyes, she stops, gulping back tears until she can speak again. "I wanted to talk to Tim big time yesterday. I rang lots of times. But no one answered."

"You knew?" I ask, feeling the worm of remorse gnaw inside me, the eerie sound of an unanswered telephone ringing in my ears.

She nods, drawing a long loud sniff. "If it was me, I would have kept him home."

I sob. "I should have stayed home. I wanted to."

"Oh, Mum. I'm sorry. I didn't mean that. It's not your fault. It's no one's fault."

We stay in Tim's bed, hugging our knees and each other, talking, and crying, and confessing to petty acts of meanness. They were all minor moments, normal family stuff. But, with no chance of apologising, our unkind acts now seem much worse.

Laura sat bolt upright and blinked through wet lashes. "I just remembered. Something weird happened last night. I felt the bed rocking. Not like an earthquake. But smooth and gentle."

"Oh, my God! Me too. At first like cradled in someone's arms. Then the whole bed swayed."

Her small voice wobbles, "Do you think it's Tim?"

"I'd like to think so, darling. Maybe he wants to let us know we aren't alone. And that he's all right."

"Weird," she said, digging under her pillow for soggy tissues. "I hope it happens again, whatever it is." For several nights unseen arms hold us, soothing us like newborns who must learn to walk again in a world with vast change.

Wanting to be with Tim as soon as possible, we arrange to visit the Christchurch morgue. "Will it be creepy?" asks Laura, her brow furrowed.

"Don't worry, sweetheart. He will look like he's sleeping."

"I don't want to see him if he's smashed up," her voice shaking.

"I know. I'm sure he'll be covered. It'll be all right."

Holding hands, we take hesitant steps into the room. Shivering and buttoning our winter coats tight, we shove our free hand in our pockets. It feels peaceful in this place that receives the dead. My nose wrinkles at astringent, scrubbed aromas, but underneath the embalming oils a woody pine softens the air. Swallowing hard, Laura pulls back. Taking her hand again, I gaze down at Tim on the stainless-steel gurney. A cream cotton shroud replaces his clothes, giving him the appearance of a dignified, chipped alabaster statue. Surface cuts to his handsome face, the only visible wounds, belie the fatal impact to his youthful body.

Laura whispers, in awe, "He looks beautiful. Our Tim, but not quite our Tim."

Contemplating my son through a blur of tears, I too think how numinous and otherworldly his physical form now seems. With acute awareness I note a curious disconnect separating what I see, from what I feel - perhaps even what I know. Stroking his brow and hair with all the tenderness I can muster, I bend over to kiss his cold cheek. Still, a large part of me doesn't believe what I see. This mismatch between my cognitive mind and my intuitive heart steps in as if to say, 'This is not the end of Tim's life.' At that exact moment I hear, 'Remember. You knew this would happen. Remember.' My memory struggles in vain to remember - something important. But what is it I should remember?

Vehicles have filled the carpark and our apartment is overflowing with friends by the time we get back. We didn't know that a photo of Tim's crash scene covered half of that day's newspaper.

"I can't believe it," says April's husband, Terry. "Tim's such a mature, responsible kid."

"He is," agrees another parent. "Often designated himself as the sober driver. What gets me is this happened in the middle of the day. Not some ungodly hour at night."

"Yeah. Everyone here knows about the all-night vigils when your kid doesn't arrive home."

"Every parent's worst nightmare."

Walking away, hushed words whispered behind a hand filtered into my hearing." Poor thing. She'll never get over it. No one gets over losing a child." Escaping to the back porch where no one will find me, I lean against the railing and howl.

It is a bewildering day. Laura and I try to mesh our old and new lives together, but our unasked-for roles are radical and raw. There could be no cosy coalescence, besides, funeral arrangements beg our ragged attention. Not wanting a priest or a church service, we rely on friends who recommend the funeral director who'd taken their teenage son's funeral several years ago. Geoffrey proves to be perfect with his openness to an unconventional funeral. Nothing's a problem, and his delicious blend of professionalism with a hint of playful irreverence brings a welcome element of lightness.

"First of all, how would you like to farewell young Tim," asks Geoffrey, "formal or informal?"

"Informal," chorus Laura, her father, David, and his sister, Ros. They look at me.

"Oh yes. Informal. He polished up for a high school ball, but he preferred casual. Baggy pants, a hoody and skateboard or surfboard under his arm."

"Yeah. He loved the sea, music and his car," says Laura.

"I shouldn't have bought that car for him." David's eyes are cast down, his shoulders heaving with emotion. "It's my fault."

We three women gather around him, begging him not to say that.

"It's no one's fault," says Laura for the second time that day. Directing her gaze at me she repeats, "No one's." Then adds, "And I want our friends to hear how he got sick. And how he recovered. I couldn't have done that. And Mum, you were at the funerals of Jess and Floyd. I want more time for teenagers to speak."

Although we appreciate every visitor, we sigh with relief to be alone at last. Our first day without Tim passes – something we could never imagine, now accomplished. Again, we sleep in his bed, burrowing into his smell like puppies in the bottom of a sleeping bag. We agree to leave his sheets unwashed for as long as possible. Laura curls up in Tim's favourite yellow t-shirt and I bundle his blue and white jacket close to my chest, savouring the remnant smells of my son. They say smell is the last of our five senses to shut down. Perhaps during his last moments Tim inhaled fragrant freesias growing wild on the side of the hill.

That night, in the small hours, something jolts me awake into startling alertness. Tim is standing next to my bed, by my shoulder. He's about two years old, adorably chubby and beaming at me. He looks so real I reach out to touch him but find I can't move or make any sound. It's as though I'm paralysed, suspended in a time warp bubble of uncommon stillness. My ears are blocked, like when flying at high altitude; it's not frightening, just strange. As if captured by a sped-up camera I watch him morphing through each milestone of his life, from curly-headed infancy to freckled boyhood, and then into teenagerhood, around the age of his passing. Finally, he matures into young adulthood, becoming a strong, young man of around thirty years old. Captivated, I hold my breath for fear of interrupting this enchantment. The scene changes and, in astonishment, I watch him shape-shift into a magnificent white owl towering over my bed. With poised slowness he raises and lowers his wondrous wings several times, before spreading his feathers to fly upwards and away. The same something that woke me sends me immediately back into sleep.

The dream impacts in a profound way. It quickens the hazy, vague 'Knowing' that Tim would leave us. I don't understand how I know this - it defies the slightest bit of logic. Yet now the idea is seeded, I feel an inexplicable sense of relief flowing through me.

Something deep within shifts, and the following days are trance-like. I feel supported by hundreds of pairs of hands, lifting me up and taking me to a higher plane. Although never consciously contemplating angels, they seem the one possible explanation for my feeling loved like never before. Like nectar, their loving, intoxicating energy surrounds me right up to the funeral.

At the same time, the elusive memory of an earlier, pre-agreed arrangement gains purchase - until an intangible part of me acknowledges I had indeed known of Tim's premature departure. In accepting this, I also accept Tim's death.

An unusual state of grace descends. Of course it doesn't erase my deep grief, but the budding promise of understanding yet to come helps me support Laura in her grief. Two versions of her mother now co-exist. One shrinking and dying, and the other sensing an awakening with quiet excitement. My heart aches for Laura who doesn't share my surrender; her sole awareness is pain.

Pressing arrangements leave no time to investigate this emerging phenomenon. We receive visitors from morning to nightfall and I am thankful for my friend Odette, who arrives without any prior discussion and moves in for a week. She takes care of the domestic stuff, providing endless cups of tea and biscuits for visitors. Never tiring in her good intentions, she tempts us with tasty homemade goodness. Our stomachs have shut down, however, with Odette standing over us, we manage to sip drinks and light soups.

Among the endless stream of visitors, one day a stranger comes to tell us she was driving behind Tim as they both wound around the bends of the steep hills. A maternal woman of my age, she softens her voice and says, "I was first on the scene, and I want you to know your son died straight away. I want to assure you he didn't suffer.

Laura and I cry with relief and gratitude to know this, it was something we had both worried about.

Weeping with us, she tells us what a profound honour it had been to share that sacred moment of a soul passing. "As I sat with him, I saw the most beautiful light leave his body. I watched it travel upwards, then stayed with your son until emergency services arrived."

Geoffrey has worked around the clock to bring Tim home to us. Following Laura's instructions, he recreated Tim's Fiat Uno, a red painted coffin complete with mock-up tyres and registration plates. We draw huge comfort from having Tim's physical, sleeping presence with us. It allows Laura and me to make a degree of adjustment, his still form filling a space that will soon become a large vacuum. His friends are adjusting too and, my heart melts to see awkward teenagers shuffle around the coffin. Through puffy red eyes they show their distress with alarming openness, other times they chatter, recalling pranks and jokes, as well as the wise and serious side of their loved mate.

Coming and going at all hours they add their signature graffiti tags and creative ideas to Tim's coffin. Laura transforms the lid with a blaze of flames surrounding a silver plaque engraved with Tim's name. It looks more fitting for a phoenix bird's hot-rod rather than his modest Fiat, but she knows Tim would have approved.

It's a miracle our blue carpet doesn't turn into a salty ocean on the days when more than a hundred people flow through our home, all pouring out their love and grief for their friend, workmate, nephew, grandson, brother and son. During this amazing time, others who knew Tim in different ways reveal new layers to us. One young teen describes how a group of friends would sit around discussing and debating a topic, a noisy affair with everyone competing to be heard. Tim would remain silent until everybody exhausted themselves talking, then he had his say. This teen said, 'He could sum up in a quiet few words what we'd tried to say for hours!'

People want to help, preferring to keep busy. I see their need to feel useful despite knowing full well that nothing is going to 'fix the problem'. Their sense of helplessness touches me as they look for ways to express their love and compassion. My brother, Stuart, gets busy hanging all our pictures on the wall. Tim and I hadn't finished unpacking or settling into the temporary new home we'd moved into a few weeks ago, and with my bed still in pieces I'd been sleeping on the floor. Somebody takes care of that too. Work colleagues from the college I'd recently resigned from arrive with an enormous hamper of food that lessens the load for Odette. What's more, management decide to continue to pay my wages for another two months, despite having only two days left in their employment. Such acts of kindness are a huge blessing.

By the fourth day, the young folk have shifted into a phase of acceptance and want to help too. After permitting themselves the time to express their feelings they are ready to look outwards again. Some are farewelling their third friend in as many months. Now they plan ways to celebrate and honour Tim's life.

A small group give much consideration to his needs in the afterlife, as the ancient Egyptians did. Tim's bright, patterned duvet cover provides an exotic backdrop against the necessities selected with great care.

"Are you sure your mother won't mind?" asks Ra. "What about the condom?"

"Nah. She'll take out what she doesn't like," Laura says as she slicks her brother's hair back and perches sunglasses on his brow. "Help me put this pendant around his neck."

"I always liked this one," Ra says, fingering the carved spiral grooves.

"Would you like it? He'd want his best mate to have it."

"Thanks. But he might need it," he replies, the corner of his mouth trembling.

Nathan places a can of bourbon and a packet of cigarettes by Tim's feet, while Ben fusses over where to put Tim's favourite CD's. When they call me in to admire their funerary work, my mouth drops open at the array of items. Tim is well-supplied with letters, photographs, jewellery and shells. Laura slips silver rings on his fingers and with a flourish places a cigarette behind one ear. Stepping back, tongue in cheek, she declares her brother to be drop-dead gorgeous.

We ensure there are quiet moments so those closest to Tim have time alone with him, talking to him, caressing him, just being with him. At such times, a rarefied air of tranquility settles in the room where he lies, handsome in his final bed.

Soaking up this stillness at the end of one day when quietude has returned, I wriggle under the gurney to write his eulogy. Lying on my belly, propped up on elbows, I review and write about his short life, realising how much he had packed into seventeen years. Even as a toddler he ran everywhere. Was it possible that on some level he had known he had limited time to get everything done? The way he overcame his conflicts and resolutions was admirable. My mind sifts through what I loved and would miss about him the most. It seems to me the important thing to him was his relationships – with himself, with others, and with nature.

We adapt to a different way of having Tim with us for the next five days. We can talk to him, stroke him, kiss him, laugh, and cry with him, and tell him how much we love him. For these five days he still dwells with us, but, all too soon, a strange transition requires us changed inner personas to step through the doorway into an unchanged outer world.

The day of the funeral arrives, and Tim's male family members and friends bear him on their shoulders down the stairway into the hearse. Taking care, Geoffrey pulls away from the apartment, but I shout, "Wait! There's Laura."

She comes alongside my window, puffing. "Mum! You locked me in! I had to climb out the bathroom window and down the fire escape!"

"Oh, my God! I'm sorry, darling. I thought you had already left with your father."

"I bet Tim's having a good laugh," she grins.

We have chosen the Lyttelton Yacht Club, right next to Tim's former workplace, to host his farewell ceremony. Throwing her heart into creating a festive atmosphere, Laura has transformed the space into a riot of colour using the club's flags, a profusion of flowers, posters, and a huge photograph collage. Her carefully considered selection of Tim's favourite music seemingly causes many parents to hear lyrics for the first time. For months afterwards when one of those songs played on the radio, people phoned to tell us we were in their thoughts. Such is the power of music. Such is the power of love.

Laura looks stunning. Her blonde hair contrasts against a bright red top, a vibrant colour emulating the blood of vitality. She honours her adored brother with a loving, humorous account of his short life. At sixteen years old, she touches the hearts of three hundred people crammed into the yacht club. Others follow, describing their relationship with Tim through words and song, each one painting a brushstroke on his brief, but rich canvas. Tim's mentor from the psychosis rehabilitation programme explains how few people achieved as rapid and complete recovery as Tim did, praising his determination and commitment.

Like Tim, I wait to speak last.

By the time the ceremony reaches closure I have shifted my attention to seventeen white roses placed in a circle on top of the coffin. Each stem rose taller than the next, symbolising each year of growth and life, creating a circle of completion.

Before leaving Lyttelton to take Tim's body to the Christchurch crematorium, Laura and I ask Tim to send a rainbow letting us know he was all right. Then, following our request, the entire funeral procession circumnavigates the roundabout at the Lyttelton tunnel entrance three times before heading toward Christchurch.

People press shoulder to shoulder at the crematorium. Laura stands close by with a friend and is amazingly composed - until the heavy gold velvet curtains slowly begin moving towards Tim's coffin. Unable to bear the sight of the red coffin disappearing, she rushes forward with hysterical sobs, her shaking body crumpling next to her brother. Lost for words, I crouch beside her and prise each finger off the brass handles, like wrestling a ruby oyster from a reluctant rock. She runs wildly though the crowd, past the two detectives standing near the door. I find her doubled over in the garden, vomiting on the manicured lawns.

Our mood sombre, we head back to Lyttelton doubtful of surviving the party. To our delight, a brilliant rainbow greets us as we emerged out of Lyttelton road tunnel. Stretched out above the harbour, Tim lets us know he is all right. Our spirits soar and we set about making sure everyone enjoys themselves as the walls of the yacht club reverberate to the sounds of Tim's favourite music.

An intimate circle of friends come back to the house with us for a cuppa to end the long day. April's husband, Terry, had known Tim since he was five years old. He'd chased him madly around his lawn many mornings before school. Usually the livewire, he shared how Tim's death triggered unresolved grief for his twin brother, who'd died in a motorbike accident at the age of sixteen. Distressed, but wanting to be helpful, he offers to take charge of the tea and coffee. Even in his solemn moments he makes us fall about laughing, when he asks in an absent-minded way, "Any one for coffin?"

Tim (17), with signature sun glasses and cigarette

Chapter 3

LIFE CONTINUES FOR ALL

*'Tim is evaluating his learning in this lifetime.
He is realising the great soul obligation he felt for
both of you.'*

My tears didn't discriminate between private and public after the accident. To them, bedrooms and supermarkets were the same. They were quite indifferent as to whether they dripped over bread or my bedspread; most people crossed to the other side of the road when they saw me coming. So, I was surprised when somebody *wanted* to speak to me, a middle-aged woman I barely knew waving out to me in the main street of Lyttelton. Her hair and skin colour, so similar to my children, warmed me to her straight away and I smiled at the approaching freckled, strawberry blonde. Introducing herself as Geraldine, she thrust a gold-edged business card into my hand. "You must see her. Ishtar is a clinical psychologist who practices as a Gestalt

Therapist. She's a spiritual intuitive. I hope you don't mind, but I felt compelled tell you." Taking both my hands, she looked me straight in the eye and made me promise to call Ishtar. Intrigued by her insistence, I made an appointment straight away.

One week later, the night before I met Ishtar, I had two vivid dreams. During one of the dreams, the beautiful face of an African boy appeared. In the other, ancient Islamic architecture drifted in. Enraptured, I walked beneath marble archways with exquisite carvings, up stairways of filigree, and into opulent halls adorned with vibrant mosaic tiles. Remembering Tim's lucid surfing dream the night before he died, I now understood what he meant by 'being there', 'living it'.

The next morning, I was somewhat sleep deprived as I maneuvered my way through a busy café that provided public access to Ishtar's consultation room, located in the same building. To my astonishment, the African boy sat at a table, and as I squeezed past, his face lit up when he saw me. Still astonished by this, I sat in Ishtar's waiting area and picked up her brochure, amazed to see that the cover image depicted the arcane architecture visited in my dream! How could this be? I was sure I'd never met the boy, and neither had I been anywhere with this type of architecture. Questions for Ishtar buzzed in my brain, more so having researched her intriguing name. With this stunning coincidence of the dreams, there were now heaps more.

My library search had described Ishtar as a revered goddess belonging to very ancient Sumerian creator gods called the Anunnaki. These mysterious people helped birth civilisation as we know it, preceding the ancient Egyptians. Ishtar was associated with love, fertility, war, plus the giving and taking of life. What an extraordinary name to have.

The concept of living gods and goddesses inspired me, and so did this modern woman called Ishtar. Tall and slender with the grace of a former ballet dancer, she exuded soothing compassion. Simply sitting in her calm presence, sipping herbal tea and inhaling the perfume of essential oils was therapeutic. I couldn't wait to tell her about my dreams.

"Seeing the boy is straightforward," she said. "In dream state you time-travelled a short time ahead of the physical experience. But I'm fascinated about the ancient temples."

Hoping she wouldn't think me insane, and encouraged by her insights, I shared the whispered prompts for me to remember that Tim would leave.

"At first I ignored the messages. But they persisted until I believed I did know. But Ishtar, how is it possible I could know that?"

"It's like this," she replied in her nurturing voice. "Your soul spoke to you this way. It prompted you to recall that you, Tim and Laura, and all your soul family agreed to this."

"We agreed to Tim's death?"

She nodded with a compassionate smile, "Before you came back to Earth for this incarnation. We all do this." Ishtar uncrossed her dancer's legs and leaned forward. "You know, I don't often see someone like you."

"What do you mean?"

"I confess that I'm a bit unsure what to do with you. I can see you don't need to be guided through the accepted grieving process. Because although it's obvious you are suffering deep grief, I also see an acceptance, even a grace around Tim's death."

"Grace?"

"I seldom see this in my practice. But I believe your 'soul' has accepted this event, and it is now your 'human self' that is having trouble catching up."

"I'm not sure what that means, Ishtar."

"Take Laura. Like most who sit in your chair, she grieves from a point of resistance. You, my dear, are grieving from a place of allowance. A place of grace." After allowing me to absorb this, Ishar continued, "It doesn't eliminate sorrow, but I believe you are undergoing a spiritual awakening. These are the first swelling buds of a potential great flowering. This is a sacred time for you if you allow it to be. Take your time." Waiting for me to dry the end of my nose and corners of my eyes, she said, "I wonder if you would be open to seeing my mentor? He could answer many questions for you. He sees everything."

"I could ask him about Tim?"

"Of course."

Ishtar's mentor also had an unusual name, someone called Raman Pascha. She said he would help me understand more about my soul and, in turn, this would assist my human side. When I asked for his address Ishtar smiled with her eyes and explained, "Raman doesn't dwell in a body anymore. Not for two or three thousand years, in fact. But he is channelled through a woman called Yasmeen."

Explaining that Raman was an ascended master, she described him as an evolved soul, one who possessed mastery of the physical dimension of planet Earth. He now existed in the realms of Higher Consciousness. I learned that he was one of many evolved souls active in their support of thousands of people on Earth, working through individuals able to channel their wisdom.

Driving home, Ishtar's suggestion whirled through my thoughts. I'd never even experienced so much as a tea leaf reading, let alone chatted with a disincarnate soul. Stopping at traffic lights, I glanced at a huge furniture removal truck in the next lane. The company name written on the side in enormous letters spelled 'GRACE'. That settled it.

Laura thought I'd lost my marbles. "What do you mean, Raman's not in a body? Is he dead, or isn't he?"

"I have no idea, Sweetheart. It's all new to me too. Somehow Raman speaks through Yasmeen. She's a channel, whatever that means."

"And we can ask about Tim? Where he is?"

"I think so."

"Right, I'm coming. Can't have you going off to see some weirdo on your own."

I noticed a little lightness in her step as she fetched her red hoodie. The braids of her new hair extension fell all the way to her waist like a strawberry blonde waterfall. They offset her creamy skin, she looked pale, but gorgeous. I heaved an inner sigh of relief, delighted we would go together.

A very normal looking woman greeted us at her door. Yasmeen looked around the same age as me, with medium length brown hair. Over her white flowing pants, she wore a turquoise tunic edged in sequins. Her warm maternal presence reassured me, and we were surprised to learn that her son, another budding musician, knew Tim. This impressed Laura, and I saw a little resistance drop away.

Inviting us to sit in her room, I took in the muted wall colours that contrasted well with rich Turkish floor rugs. Moroccan floor cushions added to the tranquil feeling. Yasmeen explained she would meditate for several minutes, allowing her consciousness to leave her body, and for Raman Pascha's to step in. "You can ask him anything you like.

Nothing is off limits, except this week's winning lottery numbers."

She settled back in her deep-buttoned leather armchair, folded her hands in her lap, closed her eyes, and took several deep breaths. Within minutes her body jolted, and she took another long inhale. As she breathed out, she leaned forwards, spread her knees wide apart and placed her palms on them. From this masculine pose, Raman looked at us through Yasmeen's blue eyes.

Moving his hands into prayer position, Raman bowed and greeted us with 'Salaam', the Persian word for peace.

Laura looked at me through lifted eyebrows as if to say, "What have you got me into, Mum?"

I confess hearing an ancient Persian, male-sounding entity coming from a contemporary New Zealand female was strange. But Raman's incredible love and compassion soon won us over. Our first session was an outpouring of intense emotions, but the second time we visited we were brimming with questions.

"Salaam and greetings. I am happy to be here to support you in this period of change. I encourage you in your need to know, and to allow yourselves to feel. I encourage you to have courage in this process of change and journey of grief as it takes its course. I encourage you, dear ones, to see the gift of this period. And to understand that it need not continue to create fresh pain. I am here to bring encouragement and support, and to offer practical help as well as energetic and emotional assistance."

Laura jumped in first with a surprising question, "Tim didn't have a legal will with instructions. Did he approve of his funeral?"

"He was incredibly pleased with your choice of music. He didn't want it to be a solemn occasion. And he delighted in learning that many remembered his smile."

"Does he mind me sleeping in his bed?"

"Not at all, dear heart. And he doesn't mind you looking through his things and playing his music. Because he knows this is how you are remembering him and grieving for him."

Bordering on overwhelm but bursting with curiosity, I asked, "What is Tim doing now?"

"Right now, Tim is evaluating his learning in this lifetime. He is realising the great soul obligation he felt for both of you. In his many incarnations, he often felt the need to protect and look after you. So, in this incarnation, it took him a while to really trust that you would both be all right on your own. You will have noticed this last year he moved in and out of this at times? And that on occasions he would go off on his own and not tell you much."

We nodded in agreement at the new level of independence which changed the former dynamics between us all.

Raman explained, "You see, that marked the beginning of his leaving. He didn't know this at a conscious human level but, at the soul level, he did."

"Ah," I said connecting some dots. "Laura moved to Mount Cook during the preceding months. Was this also part of preparing for separation?"

Raman nodded. "Indeed it was." Turning to Laura, he said, "This is part of your regret, dear one, that this could have been different. I want to say to you, there is nothing you could have done that would have made it different. It is important to understand your love for each other flowed to deep and extraordinarily strong levels. But he wants you to live well and do all the things you and he talked about. Do the travel that you planned to share together and be involved in what you enjoy. He has an opportunity to help you in your life in a way that he would never have been able to if he was alive in his human body. He can now make a difference in the way he would like to."

While Laura wept at the truth of her regrets, I asked, "Raman, was there a previous incarnation of Tim and Laura?"

"Indeed. There are many. But in a more recent life they were lovers!" Laura stopped weeping and sat up straight, hanging onto every word. "They were devoted to each other and lived in the northern part of Eastern Europe. During the time of the 1880's. They loved each other very much, but their families held different ideas for them both. They met at a young age and married in their mid-teens. It had been a challenge to declare their love at such a youthful age. But they married and bore a son, then two little daughters. Out of necessity, Tim grew up fast and took whatever jobs he could, such as cutting firewood, to provide as best he could. The generosity of Laura's family allowed them to live in her childhood home."

We listened entranced. It sounded like a fairy tale, the stuff of fantasy. Yet it rang true - it felt true.

"They loved each other so much because together they felt complete, felt whole. They were soul mates. But this doesn't mean you can't have a soul mate in this life, dear heart. Their attachment to each other grew to be extreme, and while this benefited you both, it meant that your love kept you always together. Meaning that you would go on creating the same patterns. This meant you wanted to keep making the same things happen so that you would always be side by side. Whenever young Tim investigated things that would draw him out, to stretch and grow, Laura would call him back again. So, the relationship acquired an elasticity that didn't stretch far. It became at times a detriment, but because you were so happy together, you didn't realise it." We laughed when he added, "You always knew he would look out for you. Check things out for you. Just like he checked out all your friends."

"That's true," Laura agreed with a smile.

"He questioned what they were doing, and who they associated with. Whether he was direct or discrete, he always wanted to know where you were and what you were up to. But, dear heart, he also knew that in this incarnation you needed to do it for yourself. So, at times over the past year or two, you both started to pull away over minor differences. You were beginning to see your own identity, so you could do what you wanted without him always knowing. And you kept some things from him. This signal from your soul said, 'I can be my own self, but I know that he's there.' Now, because this is such a fresh and raw process, you have been a little afraid. You felt you moved away from him, and because of this you lost him. You have not."

Laura sobbed again. Raman touched every raw point, acknowledging her deep sorrow and her regrets. But he also wanted her to fully understand the opportunity for her soul growth. And that everything that occurs is for a reason, it is purposeful.

"Your own process and own growth are so valuable, and your brother wants you to do this. He wants to support you now and will always be there when you let him into your heart. You may feel angry with him. 'How could he be so selfish and leave me, how dare he leave me!' This is quite normal. But he has always known he needed to do this. He came a little way in the journey with you to make sure you are able do what you need to do in this lifetime."

He waited for her to blow her nose and draw a deep breath. I felt her struggle to hear these words, and my heart wanted to leap in and rescue her. But I knew I must not.

"Dear heart, your brother will be in your heart as much as you let him, when you let yourself remember how much you love him. But, of course, then you will also feel where he is not. It is through your heart he can come to you."

We were nearing the end of the session. It had been tough for Laura, and I admired her courage to stay and listen. In closing, Raman said, "There will be occasions in the future when you will have very tangible experiences of him being in your company. Playing his music and being amongst his things is going to help you feel that you are close to him. This is fine by him, as long as you don't hold onto him. That way he is able to come and go. He can come to you when the time is right."

I sank back into the cushions, amazed by the incredible insight into this entrenched pattern between these two soul mates. We learnt in subsequent sessions that Tim and Laura were often a married couple, siblings and even twins. But so many entwined relationships had made it hard to tell which soul was which. This, their first incarnation apart provided valuable opportunities for Laura to step wholly into her own self, and at the same time, enabled Tim to work through us and others from the spirit realms.

At last I understood the whispered messages about remembering this agreed arrangement, albeit at a simple level, but enough to provide some relief from my sorrow. I anticipated a long journey ahead before understanding the full spiritual significance of everything Raman shared.

Laura was silent on the drive home. I wondered how she felt about this information. My relief might well be a burden of guilt for her. Would the soul agreements cause her to feel responsible for Tim's departure?

Just as we emerged out of the Lyttelton tunnel onto the roundabout, she turned to me and grinned, "Hey, Mum. That explains why I always thought if Tim wasn't my brother, I'd like to shag him!"

Shrieking with laughter, on impulse, I circled the tunnel roundabout three times, recreating Tim's ritual from the funeral procession. Doubled over the steering wheel laughing uncontrollably, it was a good thing we were almost home.

"Oh, thank God, Lulu! I worried it might be too much for you."

"Naw, it was awesome. Made a lot of sense. Though I didn't get what Raman said about the other reason Tim died. Something about him working through us and others from the spirit realms."

"Me neither. I wonder if that's why I heard those messages about knowing that he would leave us."

"Maybe," said Laura, her eyes bright. "Oh, it's so good to laugh! Let's go to the Irish Pub and laugh some more. And we can plan that holiday Raman suggested we go on. Somewhere warm, to cheer us up."

Chapter 4

BRIGHT SOUL

'You and Laura are the two most important women in his life, in his heart, and in his soul.'

Craving a deeper understanding, Laura and I returned again and again, to seek out Raman's wisdom. He introduced concepts so foreign to us we often didn't grasp the full measure until much later. In both esoteric and practical terms, during our first six months without Tim, Raman held out a lifeline. At times his words were easier to hear than heed, meaning our personalities and habitual ways of functioning often came under his scrutiny.

In one of our earlier sessions Raman, always kind, added firmness to his advice for me. "In coping with changes with your daughter, I want you to realise you must not be strong for everybody! Of course, you see the need in your child, and it is hard not to help. You desire to take away the pain. But I want you to give yourself permission to know it is equally hard for you. Albeit in a different way. No one else around you really understand how you are feeling. For this reason, it is important that both of you are supported by each other, as best you can."

And to Laura he said, "Notice your mother, and if she seems strong because she is keeping it all down, go and give her the hug she needs. Ask her to tell you how she feels." Softening his voice for her even further, "Please understand that no one is to blame for your brother leaving. You may say it was an accident, or that it shouldn't have happened to someone so young with his life ahead of him. But there are no coincidences, dear heart. Understand these things coincide for a reason. It is only then that you will realise there is a plan. To a human mind and heart this sounds nonsensical. But when you see it from a soul perspective, Tim just came for a while."

Laura's bottom lip trembled while absorbing this notion of a plan. It struck me that, although Tim could focus as a child, in the moment of completion he hurried to move on to the next thing. "He put such a lot of energy into his life, Raman. And achieved so much."

"Yes, because that's all the time he had," Raman replied.

"Funny. When I think of it, he always rushed, even as a toddler he ran everywhere."

Raman seemed delighted at this connection. "Yes, and without him consciously knowing that. He didn't walk around thinking, well around my eighteenth birthday I'm not going to be here. He simply 'knew' there was much he hungered for."

Recovered for the moment but still sniffling, Laura wanted to know, "Was there anything he wanted to do that he didn't do?"

"Yes, he wanted to tell you that he loved you more often." Both of our lower lips wobbled at this point. "There were times he did, but as a seventeen-year-old he couldn't find the words. There were times he wanted to tell you of the extraordinary love he felt. You might feel he did tell you, but for him, it was a matter of conveyance. In other words, of *how* he expressed it." Raman paused while we wiped our faces and stuffed wads of wet tissues up our sleeves.

"But he is content. Of course, at first he needed to adjust and was not happy about it all. But once back again with some members of his soul group, and after spending time reviewing, he came to understand the purpose of that incarnation."

Raman hesitated, as though waiting for permission from unseen others to share his next message. "Dear hearts, I will say this to you, he is likely to reincarnate into your family again in the future."

We jerked our heads to look at each other. Confusion and amazement at this revelation rendered me speechless, but Laura responded in a flash. "Would we recognise Tim if he reincarnates?"

"Yes. Absolutely. By his eyes. And he may return to your own family. But," he cautioned," I don't want you looking over your shoulders for him. It will be when you least expect it, when you have almost forgotten about it, that is when he will return."

In our excitement we began to babble at once. I heard joy dancing in Laura's voice for the first time since that dreadful night at Hanmer Springs. But Raman warned, "He would also quite like to be there to welcome you when you leave this world. This is something of a dilemma for him as to his readiness to return. As a soul he will review this constantly.

The outcome will be determined by the amount of work he does on himself now."

Raman explained how we would be a part of his decision making. "You see, from the soul perspective, all three of you are intricately linked, and you remain in close communication. Souls that know each other well get together in the dream state in the astral planes. This close bonding and communication doesn't take place in the same manner as for human form. It is more of an energy exchange rather than an information exchange. Humans share ideas and feelings, but on a soul level, it is an exchange of energy. When you open your consciousness, you already know everything there is to know."

We were dumbstruck for a few moments, but Laura soon collected her wits again. "Can Tim 'see' us when he is keeping an eye on us?"

"Not straight away. But as he learns to adjust, he will see things in a visual way, just as you do. At other times he is simply aware of your animation, which is the soul's energy that you radiate. He knows with the clarity as though you were a daisy in a field of roses."

Laura frowned and leaned forward towards Raman. "What do you mean? I mean, how does he do that?"

"Dear heart," smiled Raman, "your brother knows you by the colour of your aura, what you're feeling, your essence and your presence. And very often he will be zoning in on that. He's not so interested in the new things around, furnishings and new curtains and such. He's not attached to those things now. To him, you and your mother are most important. Continue to reach out to each other. Realise that you are the living link now." He nods to both Laura and me, "You hold particular importance as living links for your brother and for your son. You are the two most important women in his life, in his soul, and in his heart. His greatest wish is that you get along. Let the little hurts go. This is so important. He worries about you quite a lot, and he wants to ensure you make good choices for yourselves. He wants you to be careful and observe all those around you, notice the kinds of choices they make, and the consequences that come about as a result. This is so you can clear yourself of karmic issues, without creating fresh ones."

Turning to me, Raman shared a touching message from my son. "And for you, my dear, Tim wishes you to know you deserve to be loved. And to be loved in the way you wish to be loved, and not to let that go for a moment! He is aware and delighted that you come here and that we can have these discussions. He's a bright, radiant soul."

Raman's words brought great comfort. Yet for the past eighteen months, my radiant son had struggled to shine, at least, from a human perspective. His teachers at Linwood High School had scratched their heads and described him as an enigma - very likeable, intelligent, and creative, yet a student who underachieved.

I knew Tim grew marijuana after spotting a healthy plant growing in a pot on the roof. Much later on I realised he smoked marijuana and consumed hard liquor on a regular basis throughout his fifteenth year. When confronted, he admitted he stood on a slippery slope, but within a few weeks a different conversation took place.

"Mumsy, I've reached a decision."

"What have you decided, my darling boy?"

"I'm quitting dope and booze."

"Wow!" Throwing my arms around him, I squeezed my approval and waited for him to continue.

"I need a fresh start. How would you feel about me leaving Linwood High and starting at Hagley College?"

"Why Hagley College?"

"Well, they offer more creative subjects. I'd like to study photography. And some of my friends go there. They say it's more relaxed. No uniform for a start."

Tim settled into his new school, appreciating the less formal atmosphere where teachers treated him like an adult. His talent for photography soon emerged and, at first, he felt much happier. But within a few months, cracks appeared. Now that substance abuse no longer masked his fears and concerns, he suffered bouts of depression. He refused to share what haunted him but agreed to professional help. In private, I doubted the outcome of psychologist services, but his mood soon lifted and I ate my sneering hat. In fact, results proved quite remarkable. Sometimes Tim even spoke in an elated manner. Impressive indeed, but I also noted his new trait of impulsive actions.

"Tim, are you sure you want to sell your drum kit? And your camera? You need that."

"Mumsy. We don't need to be burdened with possessions. We should live simple lives. Man has become consumed with material belongings. Simplicity is a key to a happier life."

Our home lacked books on subjects such as Buddhism, Christianity, and philosophy. Yet he spoke torrents of information about them with an air of confidence that was hard to fathom. This new interest in world religions baffled me. His grandfather and great-grandfather were both Methodist ministers, so I didn't think his knowledge of Christianity unusual. Besides, I was delighted in this exploration of religious and philosophical ideas, it showed a maturing. In my ignorance and, yes, in avoidance, I put all this down to teenage behaviour. Until I couldn't ignore it any longer.

Our local community policeman zig-zagged his way through the packed, noisy throng at the Lyttelton Volcano bar and restaurant. His helmeted head swivelled like an owl as he scanned the room. He spotted me where I sat sipping wine and relaxing with my friends, Lea and Pav, and weaved towards our table.

We greeted him with good cheer but soon dropped our smiles. "You'd better come with me," he said to me. "Your children are outside in my police car."

"Shall I come with you?" offered Pav, but I shook my head and thanked him for the wine.

The policeman opened the car door to reveal Tim and Laura, bundled in rugs against the cold, huddled in the back seat. Tim was crying and Laura looked alert with adrenalin. I squeezed in between them, stretching my arms to encircle them both.

"I'm sorry, Mumsy," Tim repeated. "I heard voices. Telling me to kill myself. You always said to call for help. I dialled 111. They came straight away and I told them where to find you. Sorry, Mumsy."

"Darling. It's all right. I'm sorry I wasn't home. Don't cry. You did exactly the right thing."

A second police officer in the front seat turned around to fill me in. "We found him in a distressed state. I know this is a bit of a shock for you, but we're taking Tim for a hospital assessment."

Aghast with guilt, the wine turned sour on my tongue. Driving through the long, dark Lyttelton tunnel that connected our town with Christchurch, I felt small. Ceiling lights flashed at regular intervals through the window like probing accusations.

We crammed into emergency services with the Friday night crowd. After a long wait our turn arrived and following a brief consultation hospital staff pronounced Tim fit and well. They prescribed Panadol. Later, while tucking Laura into bed, she said," That was so cool, to be woken up by two police officers."

I found Tim pacing his room the next morning. Neither hot drinks and soothing words, nor Panadol could relieve the agitation that raged in him. Uncharacteristic irritability rattled him like a dry pea in a pod. Wringing my hands, recalling the hospital's reassuring assessment, I dithered before calling them. Finally phoning, I was appalled to learn of an administrative error and followed their instructions to bring him back right away.

Walking through the corridors, Tim answered each intercom message as if it were for him. "Yes, Doctor, I'm on my way. Coming right away. Thank you, Sister!"

So serious and diligent in his replies, a smile teased my lips at this comical scene while waiting for the doctor. But the correct assessment of a psychotic episode wiped away all traces of humour. Tim was seriously unwell.

"What caused this?"

"Ritalin," replied the doctor. "Tim told us he took this prescription drug."

I stared at Tim in astonishment. "Ritalin? But where did you get it from? Why?"

"From Jamie. It's not his fault. He just wanted to help. Said it would cheer me up."

Through raised eyebrows the doctor explained, "Ritalin acts as a behaviour suppressant for those with ADHD. But for someone who doesn't have ADHD, the reverse occurs. It creates a sped-up behaviour, removing inhibitors of erratic and impulsive behaviour."

Puzzle pieces slithered into place. Jamie lived on our street. A chirpy, bright kid about the same age as Tim. I knew his parents would feel terrible, we were good friends. They were proactive and supportive of Jamie's condition which often included difficult behaviour. But the blame didn't all lie with Ritalin.

"Although the drug triggered the episode, this was just the last straw that broke the camel's back, as they say," said the doctor. "You see, the combination of marijuana and alcohol compromised his immature neurological system. Our nervous system isn't fully mature until around twenty years of age. This cocktail left him susceptible to any future substances. That's all it took - a few tablets of Ritalin."

I asked for a chair, all at once feeling the weight of it. "I see. Thank you. What's the next step?"

"I'm afraid your son requires hospitalisation and treatment. Not here, but at Sunnyside."

I gasped in disbelief. "Sunnyside?" My heart sank as I pictured the grim exterior of the psychiatric hospital that epitomised Victorian asylums. Years ago I'd trained as a student psychiatric nurse in that God-forsaken place.

"Would you like one of our staff to admit him?"

"No. No thank you. I will drive him there."

Stunned at this unfolding event, neither of us spoke on the drive. At least the acute admissions unit sat in a new part of the hospital. I don't think I could have taken him to the old, brooding, stone buildings. The irony of these circumstances struck me - returning to this archaic institution with my son, at a similar age to when I had worked here. I never completed the training, being too sensitive to cope with what I regarded as insensitive, heartless treatment of patients. I prayed things were different now.

Welcoming staff admitted Tim and escorted us to his quarters for the first night, a small, padded cell that shocked both of us. A mattress on the floor was the single item, standard procedure prior to assessment of each new patient. On request, Tim handed over his belt and shoes. Terrified by this environment and sobbing with disbelief, Tim pleaded with me to stay. I did my utmost to calm and reassure him for several hours until staff insisted I go home and rest, seeing me approach breaking point.

"Don't leave me here, Mumsy. I'm frightened," he begged, panic in his eyes. His words stopped, but his weeping could not. Leaving him in that white cell was the hardest thing I'd ever done.

No longer able to conceal my own distress, I wrenched myself away. Stumbling out to the carpark, overwrought with exhaustion and filled with guilt, Tim's whimpers clogged my ears. Despair, anxiety and grief wrapped their cloak of cold comfort around me.

Tim spent several days in acute admissions before transferring to a recovery unit. For several weeks dedicated staff offered Tim compassionate care alongside pertinent information about making better choices for himself. Several months of treatment as a day patient was consolidated with exciting outdoor adventure activities to revitalise his damaged nervous system. I loved seeing him sparkle again, brimming with stories of white-water rafting and rock climbing.

BRIGHT SOUL

Following his crisis, Tim advocated using nature to experience feelings of well-being and natural highs. This was emphasised in his written reflections of recovery in the following piece found by Laura after his death. We couldn't help chuckle at the last line, his signature quirky humour we knew so well.

'I'm hoping to use my brain to make a living in the future.
I'm taking barbiturates at the moment, and I'd rather not mix my poisons.
I'm on heavy medication for psychotic episodes.
My drug addiction took over me and my soul!
I only just survived.
Do you not understand 'why' drugs like that alter your mood?
It's because your brain has heaps of 'containers'
and your brain also produces drugs of its own.
Like dopamine. Dopamine gives you a feeling of well-being.
When you take drugs like marijuana, your containers that were full of dopamine, will, now, almost be empty… because you shot bullets through the wall of your soul.
People who don't smoke have a terrible time finding something polite to do with their lips.'

By Tim Hopper, 2000

Recovery drove a slow truck back to the depot and for many months I learned to live with the uncertainty that Tim might take his life. Despite setbacks he applied himself to his healing programme and amended his lifestyle, becoming one of the few who reached full recovery from a psychotic episode. Determined to recover, he sent away for a programme to retrain his damaged short-term memory, later proudly boasting he could recall twenty items.

FLYING IN THE FACE OF GRIEF   **BY ANNWYN**

In due course, Tim stabilised enough to look for work. After trying out a few different jobs, he settled into his new life as a hammer hand at the Lyttelton Marina which was undergoing a major upgrade. Basic carpentry jobs of hammering sections of pontoons together filled his days.

"I dropped another hammer in the ocean today. That's five so far," he grinned.

"It's a good thing they don't dock your pay packet," I said.

"Nah, it happens to everybody. I like the work. The only thing I don't like is the smoko shed."

"Oh?"

"Some of the guys are foul. The way they talk about women is disgusting, Mumsy."

"I'm glad you are sensitive to that. Everything else, okay?"

"Yeah. But Johnny asked me if I'd been drinking the other day. Said he noticed I'd been absent a few times. Said I'm too old for my mother to ring in with excuses."

"I see him at the pub. Shall I have a word? Put him in the picture? He's the foreman. He'll understand."

"Hell no. Don't do that. He'll think I'm a nut case."

When Tim started working at the marina his nervous system needed more time to heal, and a fitful night left him too exhausted to go to work. He still took medication which made him drowsy at times and I suspected he got a bit of ribbing for that. No wonder the foreman thought him hung over. Not long after that, I spotted Johnny at the Irish pub.

"Johnny, could I speak with you?"

"Gidday," he said in his strong Australian accent. "You're young Tim's mum, aren't you?"

"That's right. I want to explain something. Would you give me your word this stays between me and you? Tim didn't want me to speak with you, but he's worried you suspect he's hung over some days."

BRIGHT SOUL

"Go on," he said, gulping a tall glass of Guinness. "I can keep a secret. I do have my eye on young Tim."

When I explained the circumstances, Johhny patted my arm, thanked me, and told me not to worry. Without a word to Tim or anybody else about our conversation, he shifted Tim to a different part of the construction site. Here, he worked alongside a small group of family-orientated men more aligned with Tim's personality. It provided the exact scaffolding he needed.

During nine months of working at the marina Tim grew in confidence and self-reliance. His quiet, offbeat humour was popular with his co-workers, and with his tall, slender body tanned from working outdoors, he developed into a handsome young man.

Tim beamed happiness during this time with everything slotting into place for him. As soon as his pay packet reached his back pocket, he drove into Christchurch to spend a good deal of it on clothing and music, and even a fashionable double bed. I had to arm wrestle money out of him for food and lodgings. Enjoying construction work, he decided to train as a builder. Days before his accident he approached a large construction firm asking to be taken on as an apprentice.

"Mumsy! Guess what? They said yes!" They'd grabbed this personable, strong, good-looking chap and signed him up.

"Well done, darling. You deserve it. So proud of you," I said, giving him a big kiss.

"Let's celebrate. My shout at the Irish Pub," he grinned.

He told me to order something from the top shelf and bought himself a cigar, turning green at the gills after a couple of puffs. I admired his sense of occasion.

After my second marriage had ended and our family home sold, Tim and I decided to share a flat together until we found another property. Laura already lived in Mount Cook at this time, settled and blossoming in her newfound passion for hospitality. We missed each other but the arrangements worked well.

Tim even found a way to build a bridge to his father, David. The red Fiat Uno, David gifted to Tim, became their point of father-son connection, allowing Tim to move through former frustration with his father. He often drove the ten-minute drive over the hills that separated Lyttelton from Sumner to where David lived and was driving this route to visit his dad the day he crashed his car.

Outwardly, Tim appeared to be settled. But the suicides of two friends, Jess and Floyd, affected him deeply and in the weeks before his accident he wrote the following poem. The person referred to is sixteen-year-old Jess.

'Now that nothing is real,
Why is my soul not healed?
What's in store for us now,
When her life has ended so soon?
I'm alone and must say,
No hope for better days.

It's morbid,
Full of heartbreak and pain,
My life's insane
And burns quicker.
I know we want peace of mind.
Life is weak.
It's like a jungle.
Sometimes it makes me wonder,
What keeps me from going under?'

Chapter 5

PANTRY OF LOVE AND PAIN

*'Sometimes I resisted feeling the pain.
that went hand-in-hand with feeling the love.
Unfortunately, they were stored in the same place.'*

The change to our lives feels surreal. We are reluctant to give too much attention to the fact Tim no longer lives. That he no longer occupies the spaces he used to. We don't want to make it unbearably real.

Despite Raman's words of not holding onto Tim, we cling like limpets. Wearing his hoodies, we pore over photographs and play his music while sprawled over his bed. The brand new one that I soon discover requires further payments! We read poetry in his journals and admire his artwork. Still feeling his energy as a strong presence, we soak it up like emotional sea sponges.

Everyone wants to keep him alive, we aren't the only ones hoping to find ways of staying connected.

"We'd better let you two go to bed. We've been here for hours," says Kylie, shifting her weight on the yellow sofa.

"It's okay, we love talking about Tim," Laura assures her. "Have you noticed the light bulbs and candles flickering?"

"Yeah, what is that?" asks Ra. "There's no draft in here. And I keep getting a slight whiff of something, too."

"Does it smell sort of old worldly, like incense and frankincense?" I ask.

He nods and I add, "It often happens when we feel his presence. And always when sitting around like this, remembering him."

The teens boys are our favourite visitors. Tim's closest buddy, Ra, reminds us of him by the way he dresses and smells, and the way he phrases his words. Like Laura and me, he's searching for a link to his absent best friend. We are the nearest he can get to him, and Ra is the closest reminder for us. But Ra also feels the paradox of love and pain by being in Tim's home, a place where he used to be.

One evening, I noticed had Ra left the room and hadn't come back for a while. I found him sitting on the cold laundry floor leaning against the washing machine, sobbing his heart out. Inseparable throughout boyhood, Ra had often stayed at our house, his visits punctuated by endless fits of giggles between the pair of them. At the funeral Ra had shared his difficulty making friends until the day Tim arrived at Lyttelton School. Walking straight up to him, eight-year-old Tim poked him in the chest with his finger, and declared, 'You're my friend.'

Laura, Ra, and other friends created a shrine at the crash site, decorating the rock face with painted symbols, fresh flowers, candles and even a massive teddy bear. But as the weeks went by, the young people stopped going there. And most stopped visiting us. Tim's absence filled our life. Time dragged across the clock face in slow motion. Some days we put all our energy into surviving one hour at a time.

In a tiny township such as Lyttelton, anonymity is impossible. Finally venturing out, some people's thoughts and reactions struck us hard.

"Isn't that Caroline up ahead?"

"Yeah, it is. Wonder if she'll duck down Dublin Street like the others have," Laura says wryly.

"Anything to avoid an awkward moment." I sigh, making a mental note to buy waterproof mascara.

"You'd think we'd learn in school how to be okay around grief," says my wise daughter. "What does it matter if we blub? I'd rather someone said something stupid than pretend it never happened."

"I know what you mean, darling. I hate the way people chatter about every day, trivial things."

"But to be fair, Mumsy, you don't show many people your vulnerable side either. You're pretty good at putting on a brave face." She pulls me towards a doorway. "Let's have coffee in here. Your shout!"

Laura orders our drinks while I find a booth away from prying eyes. Her observation of my role-playing surprised me - but watching her at the counter giving cheek to the barrister, I remember she'd grown up around it. And I had noticed how drained I felt when feigning happiness.

Sliding into the seat she smiles. "That's not so bad, is it?"

"Well done, little Miss Brave Face. You know what's worse than someone ignoring tears running down your face? It's the ones who *feed* off tragedy."

"Yeah, some of the girls are like that. They love the drama."

"Teenage girls can be like that. But it's the adults who revel in the emotional drama that bother me. It's as though they view me as 'that poor woman who lost her son on Sumner Road'." I hold fire while coffee cups are set down, but then my voice rises, "It infuriates me when people pity me. I won't be pushed into a role I don't want to play. I appreciate when my grief is acknowledged, but I damn well refuse to be identified by it."

"Drink your coffee, Mumsy," Laura whispers. "People are staring."

"Okay." I sip foam from the coffee. "But darling, you called me Mumsy, twice."

She looks sheepish. "Is that okay with you?"

I nod and taste salty tears in the latte.

Sometimes Laura and I visit the Irish Pub to get drunk, to laugh and to dance. To be silly and have fun while exploring the confusing facets of grieving. We still want to live life - even at the risk of a triggered moment that causes us to howl in public during this testing, exhausting time.

Understanding the noble purpose of my soul's learning the background to this event is all very well, but I often lapse into my human side, more so when tired. Since the three months of Tim's passing, even part-time work saps every drop of my strength.

One morning, I stand next to my car with arms drooped at my sides. Fatigued and resentful of the need to face the world, I allow my black leather shoulder bag to slide to the concrete, not caring if its contents spilled. My chest constricts with tension as cold misery warms into a heat that soon reaches an alarming boiling point. Without caring who heard, I rage, "How many bloody lessons do I need? It's not fair!"

Humiliated by my life lessons, my mind seizes the opportunity to re-run old stories in my head. Slumped against the car, my thoughts become a spool of old brown tape spinning recklessly around the broken recording machine before jamming into a tangled mess. Garbled voices from the damaged tape begin - I hear a small girl from a broken home asking why other kids' dads lived with them. The same small voice rails at not fitting in with her four siblings, not even her twin sister. A woman's voice bemoans the disintegration of two marriages and the struggle to raise her children alone. One of her teenagers turns feral and goes off the rails, the other suffers a psychotic episode. The tape jams and I slide to the ground.

The beautiful dreams and messages from Tim cease, and he no longer signals his presence. I feel alone again, unsupported and disconnected from him. The honeymoon with unseen loving ones is over, and I take my self-pity to Raman.

"Ah, dear heart, like you, and Laura too, your son is also getting a little busier. It is important to resume your normal lives without fear or guilt, knowing this is normal and right. When you notice that you haven't thought about him for a moment or for a day, don't feel guilty. Tim very much wants you to continue living and growing, to care for yourselves and for others. He, too, has wanted to communicate for some time, for you to feel his presence and his love. But to do this asks you to be 'in yourselves'. This is a space that is also painful.

"When you are trying to make sense of it all, and to engage in life again, sometimes it is difficult to find a balance of allowing the heart to know and remember that love, while still getting on with day-to-day practicalities.

"Healing grief is only completed when you permit him into your heart again, and when you have accepted the pain of that love. Then, you will remember and experience the joy and love from him. And that is when the door of communication is once again open."

"I guess it's when I accept the feelings of missing him, feeling sad, angry, betrayed or whatever I'm feeling. It's as though I must learn to love him in a different way."

"Yes, and by doing that you are going to allow him to 'Be' more. He'll be more open. In many ways, being the main male figure for you and Laura, was an important role. He did this in a loving and willing way, and so this is also a period of adjustment.

"You are still noticing the shockwaves and observing the new places where he is not. You will be doing something, then catch yourself realising he's not there, that he cannot be there. For just over a year, you will go through the familial cycle of life without him. It will take this long before you know where you are again in terms of him not being there on birthdays, etcetera. So don't expect to feel all right about it yet!"

Wiping my nose with yet another soggy tissue, I nod. "I guess too much, too soon."

"There is irrevocable change to your outside lives, and you are also adjusting to change within yourselves. Also, in the role he played for you both, and the love that was obvious between all of you. Although you have a sense or a feeling of him and you don't really know where he is, he is now able to be even more present for you. But if he were here, he would be getting on with his own life although, most of the time, you would know where he was."

Raman's words make perfect sense. It is *me* who has withdrawn. I have responsibilities that require interaction with the world. After all, I still need to earn money and do the shopping. When I feel worn out by daily life, I yearn for Tim's presence and love. But I know the risk I take by opening that door - pain occupies the same pantry. So sometimes I just keep the door shut. But, thanks to Raman, I now realise that means shutting Tim's love out too.

Laura's part-time return to her hospitality work has meant we spend less time together. Raman points out how our feelings, synchronised up until now, would soon change. He warns of the time ahead where our journey through grief will take different pathways, but I have no way of knowing what that will mean for us both.

"The next few months will invite focus upon your respective needs because you will both experience different feelings about Tim's death. Perhaps more acceptance from one than the other will be needed, and there are many choices and things you will feel differently about. Being aware of your feelings and the choices you make will determine how smooth this period of learning will be for you.

"True healing of grief comes about when you permit yourself to go to the place that hurts the most, because this remembering of love is the doorway to the healing and the doorway to the one you love. You will spend more time apart from Laura now, and your feelings won't always be the same, but you can still support each other as you experience this new growth."

"Thank you, Raman. That explains so much. I'm surprised at how fatigued I still get. My stamina returned for a while but, some days, I can't even get out of bed."

"This happens because your emotional levels vary. Don't push or exert yourself. You must rest, even if this means cancelling arrangements. You are still assimilating the adrenal energy that is the result of shock and grief. This is stored for a brief time in the muscles of the body. It's not until you begin to relax and begin to heal that these chemicals or toxins begin to leach out of your muscular system and start circulating through your lymphatic system. When that happens, your body must work hard. So, do what you can to help the release of these chemicals and cleanse the body. Make sure you drink plenty of water and eat well.

I roll my eyes. "Food doesn't hold much appeal these days."

"Dear heart, I have noticed your appetite is poor and you are not eating well. When you do want to eat, choose foods that have carbohydrates for fuel, and light fresh green foods, that are flavoursome but not too spicy. Your body needs nourishment more than ever at this time even though, paradoxically, you don't have an appetite. So, when you do feel like eating make wise choices and your energy levels will begin to stabilise."

"It's just so hard some days."

"I understand, dear heart. On those days when you are really down, when you are right back at the start again, do not be alarmed. Be gentle with yourself. Realise this is part of the process. Those moments when you feel raw and emotional are good times for release. Just let it happen without feeling you should be getting better now, or this should not be happening."

I sigh. "Does it get easier, Raman?"

"Grieving is grieving. And that means letting yourself mourn and be in the process. Realise that the spaces between the bad moments will get longer and longer."

Despite the love and wisdom from Raman and my openness to spiritual matters, I stumbled through recovery.

There were many days when I didn't eat nutritious food or failed to rest. Exhaustion swept over me like a road sweeper, pushing tiny bits of gravel into my wounds. At those times I felt no love, only pain.

Laura struggled too, I knew she and her friends often numbed their pain with alcohol. Her suffering was different to mine. Her grief was of a dual nature, coming from both her human and soul level. Although my challenge lay in allowance of my human pain, at least I was spared soul suffering. Tim's concerns over her well-being, and his hesitation to leave, were about to be revealed.

Chapter 6

SOUL DILEMMA

*'From a mother's perspective,
I saw how Laura suffered.
But I didn't understand
how much her soul suffered.'*

*P*eeling potatoes that neither of us will eat, I hear Laura's scream. I find her sitting in bloodied bath water, poised with a razor in one hand, shaking and sobbing.

"Mum!" she gasps, her whole chest and shoulders heaving. "I'm so scared. I don't want to be here anymore. I'm frightened!"

Tufts of her beautiful strawberry blonde hair float on top of the water and small cuts bleed at her wrists. I dry her. My little girl. Wrapping her in a thick towel and squeezing her tight, I do my best to anchor her against waves of despair sweeping her out to sea.

Now I understand Tim's forewarning for her safety. I, too, could succumb to these seductive depths. I, too, visit this dark place where tortured souls go. I, too, seek sanctuary from overwhelming pain.

Taking deep breaths until my heart stops thumping, I remember Raman's words. Without knowing what would happen, I call him, repeating his name in my mind until his compassionate nurture fills our living room. Enshrouded and enabled by his powerful love, together we create an esoteric sanctuary for Laura and myself. I hold her in this stillness until she's no longer shivering and struggling to breathe.

Laura has come face-to-face with the excruciating pain of her soul. Its agony creates enormous conflict for her human self, her life hanging in the balance. A huge part of her departed the Earth with her brother – how can she remain here when so little of her own self exists?

Our family doctor prescribes antidepressants but, after a few weeks, she flushes them down the toilet. Many times, over the years, I will marvel at her strength in choosing to stay in her vulnerable, frightening place, albeit at times hanging by a thread. Where three strands once spliced a strong bond two weak strands remained, a flimsy lifeline held by frayed hope.

One night, Laura asks me a question I can't answer. "Mum, if our dependency on each other prevented our soul growth, what did it matter which one left?"

"Can you say that again, darling?"

"Why did Tim leave and not me? I would have preferred it that way."

"I don't know, Honey. Let's leave that one for Raman. We'll be seeing him next week. Okay?" She nods and snuggles next to me on the sofa. Her inner thoughts never fail to amaze me.

Although not what Laura wants to hear, Raman's answer made perfect sense. "Dear heart, if you had returned to the spirit realms, your soul would not have the opportunities to experience what it wanted to learn - to develop into its own full potential. Your brother, as an evolved soul, understood what you needed and agreed to come part of the journey with you."

Laura shifts in her seat, frowning as Raman continues. "And there were other reasons. Because your brother is such an evolved soul, he did as much as he could in his brief period, whereas you took your time. He knew you would because you like to savour. It's not a bad thing, it's simply that between the two of you, he knew what would work well for you in this incarnation. So, he came this far with you, and indeed, he can now be an even greater support for you."

"Trust him to be so bloody thoughtful and leave me behind," says Laura.

"Ha, dear heart. Wait and see how ingenious he will be over the years - in the ways he communicates with you, and the ways he gets information across. In every way you are going to have a lot more of him than if he had stayed!"

"How is that possible?" Laura glares at Raman. "How can you say that!"

"Because, dear heart, if he had stayed, sooner or later he would have gone off on his own, perhaps ending up living on the other side of the world. And while both of you would know his whereabouts you wouldn't feel that you 'had him with you'. So, this way, yes, although he is not physically here, but through your soul you 'get him with you'!"

"But I don't have him with me," she sobs. "That's the whole point. I don't bloody have him!"

Mortified at her outburst, but in complete empathy with her, I look apologetically at Raman who waves away my concerns.

"Laura, dear, you have him in your heart. You have him in your life. He's not about to abandon you. But, as a soul, he's aware of his own growth, and his own learning while he also lovingly can support yours. That, dear heart, is how you 'have' him."

Allowing space for Laura to absorb this, Raman reveals more about her soul personality. "There are things you still need to learn in this world and, as a soul, you have been reluctant because this means testing yourself, trusting your confidence in your own decisions. This life is about living what you feel, becoming aware of your choices, and honouring them. Your brother's going to have much to say when you meet these decisions in your life. In diverse ways he's going to wave quite tangible flags in front of you! He will use people to do that, he will use physical things to do that, and at other times he will get your attention directly. He will always be there for you, in ways he couldn't have if he lived on the other side of the world.

My heart lurches for Laura; so much is asked of her reluctant soul. I'd never thought of soul personalities, but Raman assures us even our souls have fragilities. He adds that often it is the souls who love us the most who agree to play the roles that offer the hardest, but most valuable, lessons for us. At his soul level, Tim's ribboned present for her lay gift wrapped in his departure. Nothing less could allow Laura to develop her individuality in this lifetime, to step into her fullness. Aware of the determined side of his sister, he knew that given the chance, she would have followed him to the ends of the earth.

Raman's next comment helps explain it further. "So, in this lifetime, Laura, you knew you would have the benefit of someone who understood you. Even as little children you took care of each other. That allowed you both to help and support one another on your own individual journeys. However, you were not happy about accepting the 'individuality of the journey', and you didn't want this to occur. You didn't want to be on your own without Tim's constant reassurance and support, and knew, on an unconscious level that this could happen in this lifetime."

"Raman, excuse me for interrupting, but is that why Laura arrived so soon after her brother? The minute I stopped breastfeeding Tim, despite using contraceptives, I conceived."

"And what else were you aware of?"

I thought back, remembering three false labours during the ten days after her due date. "The birth delays were her soul's hesitations?"

"Indeed. It created a dilemma for her soul. Wanting to be with Tim but knowing she might have to travel this lifetime without him."

My poor brave baby. Nine months earlier she had ventured away from her brother to work and live at Mount Cook, five hours away. The original, mutually agreed intention was to stay with Bu and Brian for six weeks in the hope she would settle back into the loving, sensible girl who loved horses. And, to put distance between her and a troubled young man, Jason. To her surprise she loved the alpine village life and when the renown Hermitage Hotel offered her hospitality training, she felt grown up and appreciated. Something she had not experienced at school. Flourishing in this environment made it easier to be parted from Tim, especially after they'd had a few recent spats. It was her first taste of living her life for herself.

Since the shock of Tim's death, I'd watched her fledgling confidence ebb away. She became frightened to do things which reminded her of him, even the things she loved, such as horse riding. She said she felt so raw and open and didn't have filters against feeling super-sensitive to all that she saw around her. She missed the one person who could always cheer her up and so easily make her laugh. The one who did the little things straight from the heart, like buy her an ice-cream. Most of all she missed jumping on him in the morning to wake him. She missed having him around, no matter what Raman said about having him.

If only she could understand and accept the opportunity given at the soul level. Otherwise, a long, traumatic journey lay in front of her. While Raman shares more insights with Laura, helping her gain a different perspective, I lean back against the cushions to reflect.

Peering through a soul's lens, I searched for other signs of her soul's distress following on from her stop-start-stop birthing. She developed asthma around the age of seven years, but so did others. Then, the penny dropped. Laura's attitude to life radically changed and her outrageous, defiant behaviour began at the age of fifteen. Did she know at a deep level that within a year she would face her greatest fear? Jolted back into the conversation, I heard Laura ask Raman what her soul purpose is.

"It is good you have asked this question, dear heart. Your greatest purpose is to draw from your own self-belief. To do what *you* need to do in this life. To find your own strength and to realise the parts of you that are innately you. You see, as Tim and Laura, together you were so close, so blended, it became difficult to know who-was-who! This also occurred in your past lives together. But he will always be here for you. Your purpose is to be separate from Tim, from your mother, and to feel who you are.

"Mum's not leaving, is she?" Laura cries out in alarm.

"No, dear heart. But she has her own soul agreements that will one day move her away from you. But only when you are ready for that. You will build a wonderful resource of self that will be attractive to others. You have a main guide at this time named Jacob who is the leading guide for your soul group. He will be watching your decisions. When your choices support you, you will feel his loving encouragement. But it must be said, you tend to allow other people's dramas to come first sometimes. When your decisions are not good for you, Jacob may feel stern, and you will feel a vague sense of guilt.

"Jen is your other current guide. She played the role of your sister but died during WWII at the young age of sixteen when her building got bombed. Her guidance will help you fulfil your purpose because you have similar lessons to learn. She will learn through you because of this, and you through her. Jen's influence will be felt intuitively with a powerful sense of direction from just out of the blue. You have many skills and talents to grow and put to clever use. Make sure you always put yourself in a position where you will be appreciated and rewarded."

"Raman," I ask, "I wonder if Laura's asthma is related to grief?"

"Absolutely. Asthma is a metaphysical expression of too much emotion having to be assimilated and worked through. It can be stimulated by stress, fear, and by an overload of emotion, as well as not expressing, or being fearful of expressing the emotions."

Turning back to Laura, he says, "When you were a small child, you were so open to life, and you often took on board the emotional events occurring for others. Because you were just a little girl, you felt powerless to be able to do anything about things that you saw around you. And dust exacerbated this susceptibility. You are still a little sensitive to dust in furnishings or the wind. You will always need to take care of your environment as well as taking care of your inner self. It is your weak spot and if you are unhappy, or don't get enough sleep or nourishment, it won't take much for your resistance to fall. You need to have dust-free furnishings and be a scrupulous housekeeper.

"We all have a vulnerability which, when we are weak, things like asthma will manifest themselves. It is the body's attempt to clear out what is happening on the inside, so you will do something about it! If you injure yourself and you have no pain, you may not address the healing. It occurs at the energetic level. From a soul perspective, because the chest is all about grief, you grieved right from the beginning of this life. You anticipated the lack of support and presence that your brother would give you. From the soul's perspective you weren't happy about this at all!"

Raman stretches our emotional, mental, and spiritual beliefs. It takes us days, even weeks or months to grasp the fullness of his words. Certain aspects intrigue me while different things fascinate Laura. As we look at life through new eyes, we both make all sorts of discoveries and connections. One evening, not long after our most recent talk with Raman, Laura has some things on her mind.

"Mumsy, I'm thinking about Loo Loo. Tell me the story again."

"Here, come and cosy up. Well, it must have been quite close to your birth date, because of my enormous belly. I remember shopping that day. I wore a loose-fitting homemade turquoise dress and waddled around the toy store like a blue church bell. Tim was eighteen months and inspecting the toy cars and building blocks. But then, he spotted a pretty doll with flaxen braids." Laura giggles and sighs. "Before leaving the store I tried to take the doll from him and put her back on the shelf, but he refused to let go. He clutched her to his little chest with his chubby hands, leaving me no choice but to buy it for him. He took her everywhere and called her 'his Lulu'."

"Aw, so cute. You forgot to say that my nickname began as Laura-Loo, then became Lulu."

"Well, you know that, duh."

"This is probably duh too. But I reckon he knew I was coming."

"And I think you are spot on, Lulu. You know what else is amazing?"

"What?"

"That your body felt grief eight years before the event."

"Yip, that's amazing."

"My turn for a possible duh moment. If the body feels the future, it also feels the past."

She jostled the cushions and raised an eyebrow. "Mumsy, you are brilliant."

"Go and put the kettle on. Cheeky brat."

"Yeah, I will. But can I share something I've been kinda holding onto?"

"Of course. What is it, sweetheart?"

She chews the inside of her cheek and pulls loose threads on a rug.

"I won't be upset. Promise."

"Okay. It's not your fault," she says, "but after the funeral you got a lot of support from your friends."

"That's true. They were amazing, kind, cooked our meals and all that sort of thing. Your friends were great too, although struggling with their emotions."

"God yeah. I remember Glen turning up drunk every night and bawling his heart out. But it's what your friends said to me when they were leaving."

"What did they say?" I ask, jerking my head up.

"They always told me 'Look after your mother'. Or 'Take good care of your mother'." Her face pales as she shares this, tears aren't far away.

"Sweetheart. They didn't mean it. It's just something people say. When they don't know what else to say."

She bursts into tears. "I was sixteen. I didn't know they didn't mean it. I thought they meant it. And I failed every time. I didn't want to weigh you down when I felt really low. I tried to hold it all down. But I couldn't."

"Of course you couldn't," I say, scooping her into my arms. "And you shouldn't have to. I'm so sorry about that. Good God, you'd just lost your world, and they told you to look after the adult looking after you."

"It seemed all about you," she cries. "Did they think me too young to have feelings? To feel grief?"

"You are right. Absolutely right. They focused on me. I know your friends supported you, but they were barely coping themselves."

"And now you expect me to believe all that bullshit from Raman. Maybe when I'm older I'll understand. But right now, I can't understand why you are not angry with Tim. Because I'm fucking furious!"

'Lulu, the face of grief' (16)

Chapter 7

DREAM POCKETS

*'I feel happy on the water.
The wind blowing salt in my hair,
The boat motion deeply relaxing.'*

Laura's spirits sink like a lead sinker. She takes to her bedroom and stays in her pyjamas all day, every day. We both need a reset. Throwing out a lifeline, I book the Queensland holiday in Australia we'd often talked about. She packs her suitcase before I'd even confirmed our tickets!

Another reason motivates this escape from our harbourside village, a small town built on a crater rim. The volcano's last eruption occurred over eleven million years, but I had detected a recent rise in a different kind of activity. A tectonic shift among my male friends was generating sexual interest. An unexpected ring of fire that now scorches the groins of former platonic friends confuses and appals me.

FLYING IN THE FACE OF GRIEF   **BY ANNWYN**

Complaining to Lea and Pav while sipping wine at the Lava Bar, aptly named, it turns out my old friends had already noticed the change in the air.

"Good lord, they're like bees to the honey pot." Lea gapes, as another blue-jeans butterfly sets down a complimentary glass of wine in front of me before winging away.

Lifting my shoulders to my ears, I say, "What's going on with them? At first after Tim died, they couldn't cross the street fast enough rather than talk to me, now they want candlelit dinners."

Pav, a distinguished looking man of Romanian origins, strokes his immaculate-beard as I continue my rant. "Do they see me as easy game? Vulnerable and within their reach? Men! They're pathetic!"

"Don't be too hard on them," says Pav. He pats my hand and continues," The thing is, my dear, you smell incredible."

His wife, a great beauty in her day, nods. "Pav has noticed. It's hormonal."

"But I don't want to attract men. It's the last thing on my mind," I protest.

"Think about it," says Lea, touching my arm, "You have lost a child."

A light bulb turns on. I lean over and whisper to Lea, "My womb bled for two weeks after he died."

She draws closer for a side hug. "Yes. And now your womb wants to replace that lost child."

They say laughter is the best medicine; for Laura and me, it is screaming. We start our fun therapy at the adventure park in Surfers Paradise, shrieking our heads off during nerve-shattering rides. The most terrifying ride begins sitting high up in the air on a harmless-looking couch which suddenly plummets to the ground, stopping inches above the concrete. When she could speak again, Laura says, "That's better than sitting on a shrink's couch."

In a mischievous moment she decides to shop for clothes for Tim.

"So, who are we buying for today?" asks the unsuspecting sales assistant.

"My brother, Tim," answers Laura, her face innocent. She doesn't bother to explain he didn't wear clothes these days.

"So what size is he? What colours does he like?" she asks, as we inspect the latest board shorts and sneakers. Delighting in our dark tease, we sense Tim having a giggle with us. Several times we both feel strands of hair at our crowns being tugged, or perhaps, teased.

After two days, with our jaws sore from laughing, we head to a small seaside tropical resort north of Cairns. Even in winter we find the ocean at Port Douglas warm enough for swimming, although the locals think us mad. Raman is proved right; we had been chilled to the bone with sorrow. Sunshine and a change of scenery work wonders to recharge our depleted batteries and bring warmth to our frozen hearts.

One warm evening we pin our hair up, put on our best frocks and sip cocktails at the marina. Laura sparkles, and the dishy Kiwi barman enjoys her company as much as the only other customer and me.

"What would you like this time, Laura?" he asks, after she licks the last speck of green foam from around the rim. "Another Grasshopper?" He doesn't bat an eye when she shakes her head and replies, "A quick fuck, please." The other customer laughs so much at my shocked face he insists on paying for her rude cocktail.

Laura quickly chums up with her cocktail mixer, while I return to our hotel to sleep. I answer the doorbell in the small hours to find a sheepish barman delivering Laura home slumped over a supermarket trolley like a sack of spuds. I couldn't be cross with either of them. Laura enjoys her giddy time with new friends, saying they are compassionate, but not triggered by her loss. They want to support her in 'letting the beast out'.

Meanwhile, I'd booked a day trip on a catamaran to the Great Barrier Reef, something I'd always wanted to do. Laura's body hadn't had time to warm the sheets before I shook her out of them again.

"Hurry up, Lulu. It's time to go."

"Mumsy," she groaned. "I'll just stay here. You go."

"You promised."

"I feel like shit."

"You'll soon perk up. You can sunbathe. And snorkel." She glares at me for yanking the bedclothes off, but once on deck sunning herself in a bikini and sipping mocktails, she forgives my brutal wake up call.

Sailing on the catamaran turns into a highlight. It's my first experience on a yacht and I find the wind and the reassuring motion of the boat soothes my frayed nerves. I want to try snorkelling, but Laura refuses to come with me, so I brave it alone. Copying others, I spit into my goggles and rinse, adjust the snorkel mouthpiece and wade out into the warm water up to my waist. With my heart beating faster than normal, I decide to trust this rubbery pipe in my mouth and submerge.

DREAM POCKETS

The otherworldly beauty astonishes me. Resisting the urge to surface and tell everyone, I indulge in the boundless combinations of colours and shapes within that enchanted water garden. Imagining myself at a Parisian fashion show, I watch an endless parade of outlandish chic fishes with collagen lips. Elegant sea ferns wave from the gallery admiring those on the coral catwalk strutting their colours of sunsets and patterns.

It's the silence that strikes me the most. Although busy down on the ocean floor, the shushed, slowed-down pace excludes the bustle and noise of the outer world. Grief can't find me in such a place.

As we cruise back to Port Douglas, the wind whipping through my hair, I feel happy and invigorated. Standing up in the bow, I make a pact to take up sailing; after all, I live right by the ocean.

Back in Lyttelton, I take Tim's work belt out of my wardrobe. It still looks like new, the ochre suede feels rough to my fingers. A hammer and assorted screwdrivers fill the pockets, the smallest pocket still holding his final payslip. Into this pouch, I tuck a hand-written note asking to learn to sail. This inspired idea has arrived out of 'nowhere', and I simply follow it.

It's Mother's Day, 2001, the first one since Tim died eleven months ago. The familial cycle of birthdays and Christmas amplify his absence. Sundays are the worst. On this day of the week, I miss Tim the most ... until Grace Lowry comes into my life.

'Hi, I'm Grant. I'll take your backpack,' he says, extending a long arm. I jettison myself off the wharf and swing my short legs over the rail, wary of an inconvenient stanchion post. A huddle of three smiling faces and six arms ensured I land upright on the deck, slippery with morning dew.

"Welcome aboard Grace Lowry," says Grant through a wide smile. "She's a no-frills backyard-built 40-foot ketch." My eyes follow a plume of smoke streaming from a rusty flu protruding out of the cabin roof. I detect a little pride as he says, "And the only yacht on Lyttelton Harbour with a wood burner. She's an eyesore to the sailing snobs, but there's nothing like sitting below eating your warmed up pie on a chilly day. Meet David and Rosemary, they'll show you the ropes." He laughed unabashed while the other two drew half circles with their eyeballs.

"Oh goody, I love puns."

It does my heart a power of good to laugh and talk utter nonsense throughout the day with those good-natured folk. Like Laura had discovered in Port Douglas, new friends can empathise without the emotional triggers. They take me at face value and despite vomiting and losing my hat over the side, invite me back the next weekend. And the next, until I become a regular crew member.

Every Sunday Grace Lowry is my saving grace. The four of us would not have found much in common the other days of the week but, on Sundays, the crew hold out their arms for a hug if I emerge red-eyed from blubbing in the bilges. And they know to leave me alone when I move away to perch over the bow. Even on a good day, if one of Tim's favourite songs plays on the boat's crackly radio, it would set me off. At such times the green waters of Lyttleton's deep volcanic harbour soothes my crater of pain. Corn-coloured hills wrap their trailing golden shawl around my shoulders and secure it with a large safety-pin over my heart.

With each passing month, my frayed edges splice into a confidence that I will be all right in my new life. Standing with legs astride in the cramped cockpit of Grace Lowry, I lean my weight into the boat's motion. Nudging the tiller with my thigh, I hear Grace's immediate sigh as this minor adjustment positions her in the sweet spot. She eases over in perfect alignment with the wind and waves of Lyttleton Harbour. In that delicious moment of flirting with the wind and allowing her patched frocks to fill, the rigging stops clanging its complaints. Falling silent, she pauses as her struggle against the elements drops away into shushed susurration on the water. On cue, my shoulders drop inside my navy-blue fleece jacket. I, too, let out an involuntary watery sigh. If only it were so simple the rest of the week.

An unspoken ritual exists onboard Grace Lowry. As soon as the yacht finds her groove, David makes an awkward backwards descent down the steep, narrow stairs into the galley. There he prepares smoko after taking our requests, regardless of the fact they are always the same.

Rosemary shouts out instructions as she clambers onto the cabin top, "There's banana muffins in the top of my backpack, David. And I'll have mine up here, thanks." With a contented sigh she leans against the smaller mizzen mast, unwinds her scarf, and turns her face to the sun.

"The milk's in the front pocket of mine," shouts Grant. Tall and lean, he looks every part the skipper and, I learn, accomplished Tango dancer. Oversized, reflective sunglasses and a white peaked cap offset his tanned face. "Nice sailing," he says, stretching out his long legs. "She's in the groove."

FLYING IN THE FACE OF GRIEF BY ANNWYN

"Thanks. Hey, did you find out what those young guys were doing alongside the wharf? I saw them putting a ton of boxes into that little yacht. They were so excited."

"Yeah, I'd be excited too. They're sailing up to Opua. Then a crossing to Tonga on the right weather window. Lucky sods."

Thinking it would be a huge relief to leave my corseted emotions at the wharf, I heard myself say, "That's gonna be me. This time next year. Mother's Day. Tonga."

My brow wrinkles with this outlandish thought. How I love the winter sun warming my back and the crew's laughter that allows me to toss my mantel of grieving mother overboard. Sometimes the contents of my stomach go with it, and yet, something stirs deep in my belly. The same gust that teases the creases out of Grace's worn sails whips strands of hair around my face as though determined to flick off my freckles and limitations all in one go.

Grant glances over at me. He's heard my self-talk above David and Rosemary's banter. In a seamless motion he throws his coffee dregs over the railings and angles his head a little to one side like an owl. Making a clicking noise with his mouth he says, "I reckon you'll do it."

That night, after tucking another message into Tim's tool belt, this time to sail to Tonga, I book sailing lessons.

My sailing teacher, a seasoned cruiser, loves to reminisce about the annual sailing regatta at Musket Cove, Fiji. His hilarious stories of none-too-serious sea races and sundowners on tropical beaches sound heavenly. Tim's former boss, Johnny, offers to ask a mate, one who takes part in the regatta each year, if he knew of any boats needing crew. Not only did Johnny keep his word, but his mate turns out to be married to a family member on Tim's father's side. Arrangements were made for me, Laura and her friend, Danielle, to join a motor-sailor even though technically it didn't need crew. The salubrious vessel resembled a gin palace, with a whiskered skipper harbouring hope of a tropical romance. My defence strategy of an invented abhorrence to beards works because he refuses to shave his off, establishing a mutual standoff.

The skipper also reveals an alarming habit of climbing the mast clad only in a flapping sarong and no undies, usually when we three women were lying on our backs sunbathing. Whoever spots the ascending testicles whispers, 'turn-over-time' to which Laura would remark, 'turn-off-time'. Despite our sulky skipper we create heaps of fun and meet cruisers from all over the world. Rubbing shoulders with people who were living and sailing fulltime on the oceans whets my appetite for adventure.

Inspired by this introduction to cruising life, it seemed prudent to join the New Zealand Island Cruising Club which links yachts with crew. Through their connections I spent six weeks crewing on a British yacht, 'Sunshine', exploring the Auckland area and anchoring at idyllic places such as Waiheke and Kawau Islands. This provided a wonderful opportunity to experience living onboard for a longer period and to encounter open water sailing without venturing too far from shore. In between crewing, I worked as a mortgage broker and although it wasn't my cup of tea at all, self-employment allowed me to pursue my new-found love of sailing.

Lyttelton contained a storehouse of memories and on each return, I faced shelves of sorrow. Grief stayed close by when surrounded by the people and things that reminded me of Tim. At the same time, friends marvelled at my adventurous life and, their admiration became heady stuff for someone who thrived under the approval of others. Playing to my admiring audience and preferring adventuress to grieving mother, as time went by a brand new identity emerged.

A new name beged, and I adopted 'Corky,' from McCorkindale on my maternal grandmother's side. I loved this buoyant name, whereas 'Annette' suggested entrapment in a net of sadness - something to be pitied. I wanted to be seen as a strong, resilient trooper in a culture where vulnerability was considered a weakness. Friends and family preferred me as Corky and congratulated me on my new-found courage, my fragile state having poked sharply at their own insecurities. Cavalier Corky let everybody off the hook.

I was unaware of the monster this would create for myself, and later I paid a high price. Instead of surrendering to my feelings and allowing them to heal, I conformed to cultural expectation by taking life by the horns and giving it a good shake.

Right on cue, the universe heard my request for adventure, and an email arrived from a Kiwi skipper I'd met at Musket Cove, Fiji. Ross had promised to keep me in mind to crew on Sea Eagle the following cruising season and now offered six month's cruising around Tonga, Fiji, and Vanuatu. Within a few weeks of communicating, I detected romantic interest and stepped back. Disappointed at first, within a few months Ross wrote to tell me about a wonderful woman he'd fallen in love with, and I breathed a sigh of relief.

I purchased weatherproof gear, a lifejacket plus safety harness, and rented out my house. Our third crew member also hailed from Lyttelton, and I appreciated having a familiar face on board. It was the first offshore passage for both of us. After provisioning the yacht in Whangarei, we sailed up to the Bay of Islands and waited for the right weather conditions for our journey. True to my second dream pocket, we cleared customs at Opua and set course for Tonga - one week after Mother's Day.

Ross turns out to be a die-hard New Zealand sailor who relishes the title 'wave walloper' and Sea Eagle thrashes through the ocean for the first four days. The diabolical boat motion makes Dave and me vomit nonstop as relentless waves break over the boat, keeping us constantly wet. I take sea-sickness pills known as 'Paihia Bombs' created by a local pharmacist near Opua. They do stop the nausea, but the side effect makes me hallucinate, which is almost worse than seasickness. The moment I collapse into my bunk and close my eyes, strange images gallop across my inner vision. So begins my terrifying introduction to tripping on a yacht crashing through waves while the wind blows like stink and threatens to shred our sails. Sea sickness will plague me for at least the first three days of every passage I subsequently take until I get my sea legs, but it never occurs to me to give up.

On the fifth day we leave the notorious New Zealand waters behind us. My sea legs arrive along with warm trade winds and calmer seas that changes everything. At first, I'd been anxious taking responsibility for the boat and crew during my four-hour watch, but I soon come to relish this time alone in the cockpit. Zipping up my life jacket over warm clothing and securing the safety harness to the jackline, I sit on the high side of the tilted cockpit, fully alert. Abject fear had given way to fascination for the mesmerising lace pattern wake of the boat, moonlight illuminating each foamy frill. After settling to the motion of the boat, satisfied with the sound of the wind against the sail and the right clinking in the rigging, I look up to the night sky. Listening to Tim's favourite music in my earphones, he seems very close. In some wondrous way, he fills each star, each wave, and each gust of wind.

For a few moments I allow him into my heart - but then pain grips me. I'd forgotten the risk of allowing myself to feel him like that. I wonder if I'll ever be able to think of him and feel him around me without suffering loss and separation. Or, if I'll one day be able to hold the pain long enough in my heart for it to heal. Taking my earphones off and blowing my nose, I allow the warm wind to tug my hair this way and that before trying again, this time speaking aloud.

"I wish you were here with me, beautiful boy. You would love this as much as you loved surfing. I feel close to you here. No distractions. I see you in each star, feel you with each breeze. I hear you thudding against the hull, and I smell you in the salt air. You are everywhere I place my attention."

Emotion tightens my life jacket around my chest. It rises as a hardness in my throat, but I can't swallow that much sorrow. Instead, I howl like a lone she-wolf in the night looking for her lost cub.

Wafts of coconut oil, boiled taro, and pork drift on the wind long before we land and go ashore in Tonga. Relieved to be on terra firma for three days in the capital, Nuku'alofa, it feels demoralising to face sea sickness again on the next leg. Thankfully, this sail only takes two days to reach the northern island group called Vava'u, with its travel-poster scenery of crystal-clear waters lapping white sands. After a few days exploring the many bays, taking care to stay clear of packs of half-starved dogs and pillaging pigs, we set sail for the three-day voyage to Fiji.

Fiji provides greater opportunities for socialising ashore, and I enthusiastically rub shoulders with world cruisers from around the globe. Soaking up their swashbuckling stories of epic transatlantic crossings and nerve-wracking passes through the Panama Canal fills me with awe. It always surprises me when they regard me as inspirational for staring grief in the face and refusing to back down. "That's the spirit," they say, welcoming me into their ranks.

An amusing situation arises one day on Sea Eagle when anchored close to a village near Suva. Determined to put a reddish colour through my hair, I manage this from the small platform at the stern. Taking extra care not to get red dye anywhere but on my head, I finish by pouring bucket loads of seawater over my hair to rinse out excess colour. That evening, a deputation of three village elders visits us onboard. After chatting about general things, the conversation takes a surprising turn.

Looking at me, the oldest one asks, "Did you catch a good fish today?"

Ross and I exchange puzzled looks, and he continues, "You need permission to catch fish in our waters."

"I didn't catch a fish today," I reply.

"But we saw you. We saw you cleaning the fish at the back of the boat." I shake my head in denial, and the villager looks serious. "We saw you tip the blood water in the sea."

Blood water. Finally understanding, I salvage the illustrated cardboard packet from the rubbish bin to explain. Hair colouring introduces a new concept for them, and once they understand what they've seen, they can't stop laughing. I can imagine the story is still told in the village, maybe under the title, 'Things are not always what they seem.'

By now, Ross is missing his girlfriend. He decides to return early to New Zealand rather than continue to Vanuatu, a country I was looking forward to exploring. Plus, with my house rented out for agreed dates, an earlier arrival in New Zealand doesn't suit. Opting to jump ship, I join fellow crew member Roz, a terrific Canadian sailor, aboard a luxurious 60-foot yacht. A Dutch businessman owns this powerful yacht with its massive sails, and I lack the experience to realise we are under-crewed, even more so for racing. Our skipper has entered the annual ocean race from Fiji to Vanuatu.

Due to severe weather, officials postpone the race and, consequently the farewell dinner, until the following day. Our adventures begin right away. Despite rough conditions and not enough crew, for the first two days we lead the field. But the delayed start proves disastrous, with the kept-over food creating illness for many participants, including me. For three nightmarish days and nights, I contend with vomiting, diarrhoea, and my menstrual cycle. Reeling with nausea, I can only crawl on all fours around the boat.

I leave the yacht in New Caledonia and fly back to Christchurch to train as an ESOL teacher, which meshes with my new life. Teaching in New Zealand over the summer months allows me to spend the winter months cruising the South Pacific Islands. Corky finds happiness in her life and, bit by bit, all traces of Annette step aside.

Two years after Tim's death, grief becomes at least tolerable. Bouts of deep sorrow grow further apart and pass sooner. Corky knows exactly how often she can allow Tim into her heart without distress. But if taken unawares by his favourite songs or a strong memory, it pushes past her defence line, and Corky dissolves into Annette.

With my first sailing season under my belt, ocean passages and tropical islands shape my new lifestyle. Back in Lyttelton, friends can't get enough of my stories, and I can't get enough of their praise.

DREAM POCKETS

"Love your name, Corky. It's so you," says Debs. "Makes me think of you floating away, bobbing about on a sea of champagne. A true adventuress. I'd be terrified. Did you get seasick?"

"Every time we left the wharf. Three days of throwing up before getting my sea legs." I grimace. "The worst was during an ocean race from Fiji to Vanuatu. On top of spewing like a dog, I got my cycle. That sucked."

Deb's eyes shine with admiration, and I purr under her gaze. Her approval salves the rawness of my fledgling identity. Rubbing her balm deeper into my ego, she says, "An ocean race! You've really shown your mettle. You're an inspiration to us all, Corky."

My purring comes to an abrupt halt when I catch sight of the monster – a fleeting glimpse of the fresh pain created by hiding behind Corky's skirts. I disregard the tingling sensation at the top of my head. Too late. The monster already roams. Searching for distractions that devour grief and fragility, the beast well understands this unspoken collusion. It recognises and supports my invented Corky, this swaggering new self that allows her and others to dodge despair.

Ignoring my inner voice of disquiet, I dial up bravado and respond to Debs in a rush, "Oh, it's really nothing. Imagine sailing around the world, Debs. That's what I really want to do. It sounds weird, but I've already written that dream in a note to Tim."

"Tell me more, Corky," she says, with an emphasis on 'Corky.'

"I still have the toolbelt he used to wear at the marina. I use it as my dream pocket. Like I did when I wanted to sail on Lyttelton Harbour, and then to sail to Tonga."

"That's it? That's all you did to get to Tonga?" Deb's eyebrows knit in a perplexed pattern. I note a dropped stitch.

"I'm a practical dreamer." I laugh. "I also joined the New Zealand Cruising Club and made myself known to skippers that way. Then I pictured myself sailing to Tonga, standing on deck under the stars with flying fish landing at my feet. I felt the exhilaration of already doing it. This time, I'll wait at Opua and see what magic happens."

"How did you know to do this?" she wants to know.

"I can't really say. The idea just occurred to me, but I think Tim might have something to do with it," I say and wink at her.

"Is this what they call trusting fate?"

"I think I'm learning to trust life, Debs."

Laura, now eighteen years old, has resumed her work in hospitality in Christchurch. Her world continues to be shocked by deaths in her circle of friends through accidents, illnesses, and suicides. Over the following decade, she experiences the loss of ten more friends. However, we also frequently sense Tim around us, announcing his presence in humorous ways. I often find the rearview mirror in my car turned up toward the roof. I can imagine him saying, "Look up, Mumsy. Move forward, don't look back."

Now fully identified as Corky, the adventuress, my ambition to world cruise feels like a distinct possibility. In fact, I add another request to my dream pockets, stating my desire to enter into a relationship, not just sail as crew. Heaven only knows why I feel ready to give my tattered heart to another. Although I've never heard of creating your own reality or how to manifest your dreams, I instinctively do this — it feels right. I update my desire and store Tim's toolbelt away again, leaving my wish in the hands of the universe.

DREAM POCKETS

A few months later, while visiting Auckland, I pin up a crewing offer on the message board at the Westhaven Marina. Grunting to push the thumbtacks in, another message catches my eye — that of a German skipper looking for a female crew member to sail to the Islands. I jot down the number. That evening, I make the phone call that will catapult me into one of the most extraordinary parts of my life, including finding out who Corky really is, or rather, who Corky really isn't.

Chapter 8

SOUL MATE - SHIP MATE

Manny, "I wonder who Corky really is?"

I narrow my eyes, anxious for my first glimpse of Manny. Heat smothers the cabin the moment the tiny inter-island plane touches down in a cloud of dust at Savu Savu Airport, Fiji. Peering through the small, crackled window, I spot him towering over the others. He'd told me about his basketball days in his youth. Wearing a faded orange t-shirt and khaki baggy shorts, he looks like a typical cruiser from this distance. We've shared an enormous amount of information, communicating via email over several months and, although I've gained a good sense of him, over the next ten weeks I will soon learn he's anything but typical.

The reality of meeting this man in the flesh for the first time suddenly feels reckless. Buoying myself up with bravado, I determine to guard against uninvited fears or doubts sneaking in. Excited, I unclick the seatbelt and cross my fingers, hoping this meeting will go better than the last one.

A misunderstanding had aborted our first attempt. Somebody once told me the dynamics of a new relationship reveal themselves within the first six weeks. Several degrees of truth lie in that decree. Some months ago, with hopes of sailing to Vanuatu for the 2003 cruising season, I had responded to Manny's search for crew.

His deep, calm, yet playful voice at the end of the phone creates my first impression and is the aspect I fall in love with. "Have you sailed to Fiji?" he asks in his soft tone.

"Yes, last year. I sailed the milk run."

"The milk run. What is that?"

"It's the name Kiwis give to the circuit from New Zealand to Tonga, Fiji, New Caledonia, and back to New Zealand." I like his hearty laugh.

"The milk run. That's so Kiwi. And you went to all those places in one season?" He continues talking before I can reply. "Well, I'm different in that way. I plan to spend the entire five months in Fiji. I don't do the milk run."

"Oh, that's a pity. I hope to explore Vanuatu this year," I say, pulling his huskiness into my ears.

"But there's much more to discover in Fiji. We would sail to Vanua Levu in the north and visit the out-of-the-way places that yachts don't often visit. It would be adventurous," he coaxes in his low rumbling German accent. I like the way he sucks air between his teeth as he articulates each 's' that becomes a 'z' in his language.

We chat with uncustomary ease, but with my sights set on Vanuatu, I decline joining him. However, it's not easy to dismiss a call with destiny. Reflecting on our conversation that night in bed, I wonder if I'd acted with haste. Manny's voice drew a strong, immediate attraction. It held a gentle reassurance and self-confidence that warmed my heart. During our conversation, a blurred familiarity had arisen from deep within me, as if we already knew each other. Besides, unlike most cruisers, he'd been honest, saying he hoped to meet someone for a relationship. After all, he could sail single-handed if he wanted to. My dream pockets contain my hopes of sailing the world with a partner, yet I dismissed this very opportunity with coolness, deeming it the wrong Pacific package. I call him back first thing the next morning.

During weeks of animated phone conversations, Manny reels me in until I agree to a fortnight trial sail. A test run feels prudent before committing to sailing offshore, and the proposed dates coincide with completing my first teaching contract at a Christchurch international language school. I will be free to cruise over winter, a practical motivation when choosing this change of career. The following weeks pass with mounting excitement as we plan our initial cruise to Great Barrier Island, a day's sail from Opua.

My flight to Auckland and bus ticket to Opua are booked and bags packed when Manny calls me. I hear his anger for the first time. "I read your advertisement on the marina notice board today," he snarls down the phone. "Are you looking for a better offer?" His bite sends shockwaves through me. "I've met women like you before. Always jumping from one yacht to the next. Always looking for better prospects."

"What? Wait. No, please listen." My voice shakes as I struggle to gather my wits. "Manny, it's just my old notice. That's all."

"No! It's new. It's just been posted. I pass that board each day. I should know," he hisses. The buzz of his abandoned phone flows into my hand, a fistful of dreams droning.

FLYING IN THE FACE OF GRIEF **BY ANNWYN**

I struggle to think straight in a fog of intense feelings. After a couple of days racking my brain trying to work out what happened, I remember. I'd asked a friend some weeks earlier to post my notice at the Opua Marina upon his arrival. I realise now he must have just arrived and posted my redundant message for me. Elated, I call Manny's mobile, anticipating a good laugh over our tiff.

"Manny, I know what happened. It was a simple mistake, that's all."

"Do you take me for an idiot?" he jeers. "Don't play games with me."

His refusal to be placated by the truth descends like a blanket of low cloud. "You don't believe me. You think I'm a liar." I pause and inhale for strength. "Well, stuff you. You stupid, stubborn kraut!"

At first, exasperation turns into relief. But soon, our unpleasant parting words haunt me. Destiny's bell still rings in my ears. I replay our delightful exchanges in my head, savouring the voice that magnetised me. No longer able to ignore the insistent desire to make peace, I draft an email of regrets, apologising for my vitriol, and suggest we part on good terms. To my surprise, Manny, now in Fiji, answers straight away. Although he doesn't apologise, he also regrets the incident and surprises me again by resuming communication. Our earlier disagreement would foreshadow the future nature of our relationship but, of course, we couldn't know that at the time.

A new level of gentleness enters our friendship through emails crossing the ocean each day between New Zealand and a remote part of northern Fiji. We go deeper, sharing our philosophies, beliefs, and life stories. I learn that Manny's former wife fell in love with the voice of another yachtie over the cruising network radio to the point of obsession. I also discover that, within the cruising fraternity, some women indeed determined careers by upgrading skippers as better prospects arise. No wonder my late-posted message on the notice board triggered him.

After a couple of months of communing, the potential for a relationship and global cruising appears in our binoculars. Together, we possess 20/20 vision of a shared future, and to my utter joy, Manny issues an invitation to join him. Aware of the feelings I've developed for this charismatic man, I accept. Another materialisation of my pocketful of dreams. Could Tim have lent a hand in this?

Manny bends his head, and I stretch up on my tiptoes to return his first kiss. In those first crucial moments, we both laugh, heave huge involuntary sighs of relief, and laugh again. Although noting that this first physical encounter sparks the familiar tingling sensation around my crown, I'm surprised at how soon I feel at ease. A taxi appears and we chat all the way to the Savu Savu Marina, where Kaleidoscope awaits us.

Manny confides that his mouth fell open at his first sight of me. Though our long-distance relationship revealed our mutual playfulness, he didn't expect to see a 'sexy woman' walking across the red dirt tarmac. I had emailed photos, but perhaps his overriding perception imagined a middle-aged, grieving mother — not at all sexy. Flattered by his reaction but knowing his aversion to social-climbing women, I detect a slight unease with his glamorous new girlfriend.

"So, I wonder who Corky really is?" Manny asks with an amused smile as we leave Savu Savu Marina and move into the Soma Soma Straits. I turn away, looking back at coconut trees and thatched bungalows dotting the shoreline as his words flutter through my belly. Heading toward a remote

FLYING IN THE FACE OF GRIEF   BY ANNWYN

village past Viani Bay, an easy day's reach, I manage not to throw up on our first sail, maintaining my sexy, wanderlust image.

Perched on the cockpit rail, jaunty in red shorts and a white shirt, I steal looks at the strong, tanned man at the wheel of Kaleidoscope. His strong physique reinforces a palpable sense of self-empowerment that both comforts and unnerves me. At 5 foot 3 inches, I would fit neatly under one armpit. No doubt I could have nestled there, held secure in his strong self-assuredness, but I suspect my own scattered self-worth would have become an irritant. A man of the world like Manny would soon scratch at my insecurities like an infestation of grieving, menopausal fleas.

Kaleidoscope looks just as Manny described. A far cry from Grace Lowry, this medium-sized, 46-foot French ketch bears a wide beam to keep her stable in rough seas. Two masts allow Manny to hoist and lower smaller sails with ease, and everything onboard appears well-maintained and shipshape. I feel safe. Below deck, a spacious saloon and two cabins gleam with varnished timber floors and joinery. Tasselled Indian cotton cushions are scattered over blue wool-covered squabs, matching the curtained windows that let in light. I admire the comfort created within Manny's practical floating home — it reflects a favourite maxim from my former career in interior design: 'One should possess items both beautiful and practical in one's home.' Yacht-scale living suits my stature but, occasionally, Manny fails to duck beneath solid ceiling beams, and I hear him mutter, "Scheiße!"

Cruising alone in this remote part of northern Fiji for many weeks, Manny had befriended a cluster of villagers who live near a sheltered anchorage. Having promised to bring provisions back from Savu Savu, he takes care loading two sacks of flour and rice into the rubber dinghy, ensuring the floor is dry. Taking our time, we motor through a surreal mangrove of briny, green water, navigating roots, trunks, and thick coils of hanging vines. Reaching uneven, long-grassed land, Manny heaves a bulging sack over each shoulder. Spotted by the children first, shouts fill the air, and men run to take the sacks from Manny's sweating back. Their warm welcome speaks of the big impression he's made on this little community, the chief greeting him as his honorary brother. My welcome holds less zeal. Disappointed looks on two of the women's faces suggest hopes were building around this single man who had lived among them for the past two months.

One of the hopefuls happens to be the chief's sister. "How long are you staying?" she inquires.

"Long enough to catch a prawn," I joke.

This meets with loud laughter and approval. With dashed hopes set aside, a group of women invite me to catch freshwater prawns and wash clothes together the next day. I prove hopeless at both tasks.

Saying goodbye to polished nails, I stand in the muddied waters, groping beneath slimy weeds and shrieking at the first thing that wriggles. Standing with their hands on their child-bearing hips, the women look on with disdain at my pathetic attempts to thrash t-shirts on the rocks. It must perplex these strong, practical women that Manny would prefer a squeamish weakling to one of them. I stomp barefoot around my basin of sudsy water, describing how soap powder works, causing gales of laughter. They insist on washing Manny's clothes again, attacking each item with coconut soap and a nylon scrubbing brush. Coming across a pair of my brand-new undies, a discreet examination takes place before they whack them with vigour on the rocks. I smother a giggle, suspecting Manny, like a prawn, has wriggled out of a tight squeeze.

It's naive to imagine living on a yacht to be the ultimate dream when cruising life contains a paradoxical mix of freedom and confines. I soon discover that my perception of Manny's chilled persona is as accurate as sexy Corky. Below his calm appearance lurk uncharted reefs that I bump into, not recognising them as my own rocks of resistance. During our first weeks together on Kaleidoscope, we ride wild waves of emotional peaks and troughs, discovering each other's strengths and fragilities.

There is no time-out room onboard a yacht, and there is no secret place to stash one's sack of societal conditioning. Instead, they jostle below deck like badly stowed provisions, until they spill out, knocking into each other. Within this passionate, 24/7 environment that rules out time alone, we lay the foundation stones of our relationship.

Having sailed with New Zealanders and Brits, I feel comfortable around their casual ways and thigh-slapping humour. Manny, by contrast, values caution and subtlety of wit. A seasoned sailor with a sound understanding of weather patterns and cycles, he holds zero tolerance for unnecessary risks. After all, for many years, Kaleidoscope was home to his wife and two children. I appreciate this, having endured unpleasant ocean crossings where egos overrode safety or when computer-generated forecasts placed too much faith in technology. To rail against his absolute authority in all domains of yachtsmanship would be foolish, but I challenge what I assume are negotiable day-to-day matters, such as cooking. Already an accomplished cook, I soon adapt to the compact galley, with its hob top swinging in rough seas. In this domain, I want to wear the apron of authority. Manny's simple but tasty cooking revolves around one-pot-wonders. I know Manny to be a kind man but, unlike his gimbal-mounted cooker, he maintains fixed boundaries.

"How about pumpkin risotto for dinner?" I suggest.

"Sounds wonderful, Sweetie Mouzee. But pumpkin stores well. We should eat the cabbage first."

"I agree it keeps well. But we could begin with risotto, have cabbage tomorrow, and then go back to the pumpkin. I have a great soup recipe."

"Sweetie Mouzee, we should eat the cabbage first. It makes sense."

"Okay, coleslaw it is. By the way, would it be possible to store the spices where they're easier for me to reach? I use them all the time."

"Ah, Sweetie Mouzee. I already took a lot of care planning where everything should go. The spices are perfect where they are."

"Yes, but they are difficult for me to reach. And I enjoy working in the galley more than you."

"That's true, Sweetie Mouzee. But they are in the ideal place."

Although our disagreements are over minor things, Manny always finds a sound reason for not making changes. My empowerment wilts. On land, I enjoyed independence and could hop into my car, going wherever I liked at any time. But the outboard motor on the dinghy embodies Manny's resoluteness – I find it difficult to start up. This makes me reluctant to go ashore alone, in case I can't get back to the boat. Resenting my curbed ability to come and go as I please, I begrudge Manny for having a stubborn motor. How I long to ring a girlfriend and complain about the unfairness of life.

FLYING IN THE FACE OF GRIEF — BY ANNWYN

To describe Manny's selfish, domineering ways, and how unappreciated I feel! But there I am, on a gorgeous yacht in a beautiful, remote part of Fiji, with nowhere to hide my sense of smallness.

Manny's memory for every spoken word astonishes me, and any careless half-truths come back to bite. It isn't dishonesty that I hide behind but a conditioned response to a role assigned by my mother. Overwhelmed with five children all under the age of five, she had relied on me not to add to her troubles. This acquired default setting of peacemaker conceals what I think and feel to maintain harmony in personal, professional, and community relationships.

By contrast, Manny had grown up in post-war Germany with parents who experienced the consequences of skilled, manipulative orators. They instilled in their children the ability to detect any hint of dishonesty or lack of integrity. My protective habits of double-speak and witty throwaway comments hit a raw nerve, and he challenged me to my core about this. Manny refused to recognise 'Corky', never calling me that. Determined to find out who Corky really was, he set about dismantling my constructed scaffold of concealment, layer by layer.

One evening, we sit outdoors, sipping rum and coke on deck, watching the sun dive behind the horizon as though in a hurry to finish its day. With legs stretched the width of the cockpit, Manny smiles his slow, lazy smile and says, "Sweetie Mouzee, in Germany, we would say you are a flirt."

"Nonsense," I say, through a handful of salty peanuts in my mouth. "Flirting is just being sociable. It's a cultural thing. New Zealanders are known all over the globe for their friendly, helpful nature."

"Sweetie Mouzee, I grew up in post-war Germany. I have an inbuilt bullshit detector."

I shrug. "I can't help it. It feels natural to be pleasant."

"And is it natural for you to please people you don't even know?"

"I don't know what you mean," I say, stung.

"Sweetie Mouzee, you have an erroneous need to make people like you. More than that, you seek their approval."

"You don't care what people think about you?"

"No, sweetie, I don't. I don't need anyone's permission to be who I am. Even when some people call me arrogant."

"They are right, you are arrogant," I snap. Taking my rum and snatching up the bright pink parrots on my flowing sarong, I carry my deflated feelings to the stern. I consider clambering down into the dinghy to put extra ropey meters between us. It's common to see someone trailing a few meters behind their boat. Making a rum choice, I nurse the glass I don't want to spill.

Sulking at the back of the boat with my bare feet on the swimming ladder steps, the warm evening breeze tugs at my parrots, coaxing them to fly. A part of me knows I should release these outdated beliefs I hold onto, but I don't know what to replace them with. I know I've invented Corky, but I also know I no longer identify with the woman, wife, mother, teacher, friend, community volunteer, the one first to put her hand up and insist on taking the extra roster, bringing the morning tea, baking for the cake stall, forgiving a disloyal partner. The one that carries a doormat over her shoulder instead of a handbag.

Nobody tells me the wingtips of grief reach into every pocket, searching for crumbs to feed a starving heart. Nobody sits me down and warns that grief will seek out every unloved part of me or that every morsel that doesn't taste good enough will be spat out. But the moment I sense this for myself, I draw a bolt across my heart and give Corky the key. Now, Corky won't give it back.

At other times, Manny and I are in total sync with each other. In those moments, we share a deep, respectful love in absolute harmony that feels rare. Sometimes, when snorkelling in Fiji's gorgeous underwater gardens, Manny cradles me in his underbelly. His long arms wind around me, powerful legs kicking through the warm waters. Secured in the embrace of my adoring lover, I surrender to the passing scenery of colourful fish and corals. Sometimes he feels like a caring big brother and sometimes like a distant, disapproving father. Like a petulant pendulum, I swing from loving him to hating him, depending on which lens I'm looking through at the time.

The mental and emotional tension of adjustment takes its toll, and we both go down with the flu. Unlike the usual shore-based courting process of gradually spending more time together, we have become the sole focus of each other in circumstances that excludes all other aspects of our lives. Our bodies signal time-out, and although Manny had secured a place in my heart, with a sense of shared relief, we agree I will fly back to New Zealand.

As fate would have it, within hours of booking my flight to Auckland, I spot an interesting notice on the information board at Savu Savu Marina — a cruising couple advertising for someone to teach them English in exchange for free passage on their catamaran. I bump into the skipper, Ricardo, while reading his notice. He signs me up straight away in true Italian macho style before even meeting his wife, Alina, who hails from Uzbekistan. Lucky for us all, love strikes at first sight, and I join this delightful couple for six fabulous weeks of circumnavigating Fiji. Their light-heartedness provides a perfect tonic after the intense time onboard Kaleidoscope with Manny. Ricardo makes wonderful flatbreads and maintains an impressive batch of homemade beer on the bubble. Each morning after breakfast, I teach a grammar lesson in the cockpit and, throughout the day, create informal opportunities for them to practice that point of grammar. They teach me a thing or two as well.

The spiky nature of Ricardo and Alina's relationship fascinates me; they seem comfortable with a constant low level of conflict. Every so often, a valve opens to let off steam, after which they soon make up. They teach me that the world doesn't fall apart when they are honest with each other. Alina, a witty, willowy blonde, reveals her talent as a storyteller. Her natural flair for story, combined with charming blunders in English, leaves me in stitches. My favourite tale involves Alina's grandmother's dog, a small, white, shaggy breed with fur straggling down over his eyes. As a little girl, Alina grew concerned about his curbed vision and trimmed the overgrown fringe with her grandmother's scissors. Unused to direct light, he found his own remedy—a heavy brocade tablecloth edged with a deep tasselled fringe covering the grandmother's dining table, draped at just the right height for him. He would stand there for extended periods with light filtering through the tassels until his fringe grows back.

With my batteries recharged, I fly back to Auckland. Ricardo connects me with a large Italian yacht with an international crew, which provides passage back to Opua Marina in the Bay of Islands. Again, in exchange for lessons. Although the owner speaks five languages, including English, the Kiwi accent baffles him.

Meanwhile, Manny also returns to Opua. No doubt time alone on Kaleidoscope and the smooth passage rejuvenate his depleted energy too. His face lights up in pleased surprise when I find Kaleidoscope's marina berth. Although we had parted as friends in Fiji, uncertainty prevails. The depth of our feelings for each other overwhelms us, as does the intensity of our conflict but, after a brief period of cautionary shyness, we agree to reconnect after my visit to Christchurch. I need to see Laura and refill my purse with another summer teaching contract.

Over the autumn months, we explore walking tracks in the far north region of New Zealand, sharing a camper van, an even smaller area than Kaleidoscope, with surprising harmony. This time, I tease Manny about his scientific, over-thought list of what goes in his backpack, right down to the last weighed apple. We are on terra firma, doing something I know a lot about, boosting my empowerment again.

A medical prognosis of cancer at first shakes my regained confidence, and it's a relief when further tests declare me fit and well. But the lengthy diagnostic process makes us miss the window of favourable conditions for a safe ocean passage. Many skippers would take that risk; instead, Manny seizes the opportunity to fly to Germany to settle financial affairs.

During his two-month absence, I live onboard Kaleidoscope at Kerikeri Marina, experiencing living alone for the first time. Kerikeri lies on the east coast of Northland's scenic Bay of Islands, and each day I relish a contemplative walk along beautiful coastline or through lush native bush bursting with birdsong.

Baking, cooking, reading, and sewing help fill my time and, at first a little lonely, I come to cherish silence and peace. It's a new experience to be content on my own, happy in my own company. All the while, I maintain close contact with the soothing element of water that I find profoundly healing. Realising I no longer rely on others and the constant busyness of life to fulfil me, I practice the gentle art of 'just being', rather than 'doing.' This time of solitude and self-nurture presses a restart button, setting the course for an inner journey home, home to a peaceful place within myself. How ironic that during this non-sailing season of 2004, with strong ropes attaching Kaleidoscope to a marina berth, my epic voyage towards freedom begins.

Chapter 9

ROCKING THE BOAT

'Like the sea bird, I try to perch on a shifting target.'

*K*aleidoscope gleams with fresh varnish and new paint. We have used our time in New Zealand well, hauling her out of the water to clean and repaint her hull. Occasionally, needing a break from the noisy sanding machines and toxic chemicals in the small Opua boatyard, we pack a campervan and explore different parts of Northland. By the time the cruising season begins in May 2005, Kaleidoscope has never looked better, and her occupants have never been happier. Manny and I drive with excitement to the Whangarei supermarkets and specialty shops to purchase six months' worth of provisions in one spree. It takes us a couple of days to stow the supplies in the bilges and other awkwardly reachable cubbyholes.

Eager to leave New Zealand waters, we plan to divide the next six months between southern Fiji and Vanuatu. But Fiji

FLYING IN THE FACE OF GRIEF BY ANNWYN

holds much to discover, and we love to take our time. Before we know it, we have spent our entire time there and now the South Pacific cyclone season draws near. It's time to think about our return passage to New Zealand once the unsettled September equinox passes. Vanuatu will have to wait until the following season. Over these past months, we have dived even deeper into our loving relationship, although we still find barnacles that need scraping now and then.

Basking in our newfound level of harmony, we decide that rather than return to New Zealand, we will sail north — first to Kiribati, then onward to the Marshall Islands in the far-flung reaches of the North Pacific Ocean. From there, we can sail south, spending the cruising season in Vanuatu before returning to New Zealand. Excited about our upcoming adventure, we make our way to Vuda Point Marina, where we can purchase provisions at nearby Nadi for another six months. We also need yachting services to equip Kaleidoscope with improved refrigeration for equatorial conditions.

After a flurry of activity, we are a few days away from undertaking the long passage from Fiji to Kiribati when unexpected news arrives from Laura via sail mail.

"Aren't you thrilled to be a grandmother, Sweetie Mouzee?"

"Manny," I sob, "you don't understand. This is the same boy I dragged her away from six years ago. He's the reason I sent her to live with my friends in Mount Cook — to keep her safe."

"But she is twenty-one now. A young woman."

"A young woman escaping crippling grief through drugs and alcohol. And a young man damaged by his unstable upbringing. He's the last person who spoke to Tim, did you know?"

He shakes his head, worry creasing his brow, his antennae already twitching. "What will you do?" he asks.

"Things will end badly. I must encourage her to leave straight away."

"She won't, Sweetie Mouzee. Not if she loves him."

"Will you take me ashore? I need cell coverage."

My rehearsed speech flies out the window the moment I hear her voice.

"Laura, it's me."

"Mumsy! Did you get my news?"

"I did, sweetheart."

"Are you excited about becoming a grandma?"

"Darling…" I hesitate, reluctant to burst her bubble. "I'm sorry. I know you are thrilled, but have you thought this through?"

"I haven't used drugs for a while now." She pauses. "Oh, here we go again. It's because of Jase, isn't it?"

"I know what it's like bringing up children alone, Laura."

"I won't be alone. He's changed, Mum."

"Is he working?"

"No, but…"

I cut her short. "Laura, you are paving a difficult path for yourself."

My phone buzzes in my ears. She's hung up, and I burst into tears. Manny looks worried, sensing my quandary. Throughout my life, I have managed to please and support everyone, even when it compromises and exhausts me. I fret, unsure how I can please the two people I love most. Our major sailing plans and absence from New Zealand for another twelve months mean I won't be able to support Laura at all. I know from his track record that she is unlikely to receive support from Jason. Through my solo mother lens, I foresee a difficult future for her and her child.

Recognising my dilemma, Manny struggles too, knowing it could alter our plans. After giving our predicament some thought, he suggests, "Sweetie Mouzee, we could sail to Australia instead."

"Australia? Why would we do that?"

"There are good reasons. It would be much easier for solo navigation, and easier for you to reach Laura from there."

"That's good thinking. And you are right on both counts." Hesitating I add, "But do you really want to sail to Australia? When have you dreamed of cruising the Marshall Islands?"

He lets out a long sigh and places his paddle-sized hands on his thighs. "To be honest, no, Sweetie Mouzee. It's not my first choice."

"I didn't think so. I appreciate your kindness. I do. But, you know, Australia doesn't ring my bell either."

"I would need your help navigating the Marshalls, Sweetie Mouzee. There are dangerous coral reefs — uncharted and difficult to see." The fan blows a contemplative silence around the saloon. The coolest part of the boat, I don't want to heat it up with an argument.

Moving closer to Manny on the couch, "Manny?"

"Yes, Sweetie Mouzee." He puts his arm around me.

"We should go north. Our relationship comes first, and Laura must make her own decisions."

"But you won't be able to help her," he warns.

"I must trust her," I say, feeling my voice sucked into the whirring fan. "We go north."

Telling myself I can live with my decision, I ignore my internal dialogue, unaware that I have sown seeds of resentment. I feel forced to choose between Manny and Laura when, in fact, nobody is forcing me to do anything. My old pattern of pleasing everybody menaces, causing guilt for not supporting my daughter. No matter how hard I try to shake off this habit, being rooted in lack of self-worth it puts up serious resistance. Regrets and emotions plague me as each nautical mile takes me further away from her. My silent resentment grows like an invasive weed that threatens to strangle the beautiful flowers in our relationship.

It is now October 2005, and we are well underway. Our first destination, Kiribati, lies two thousand nautical miles ahead of us. Kaleidoscope will pass through a convergence zone where the two weather systems of the South and North Pacific oceans meet. Anything can happen in this area, from roaring winds and high seas to dramatic electrical storms, or even the absolute calm of the dreaded doldrums. I too, am notorious for being unpredictable.

In many ways, the convergence zone mirrors the polarities onboard our relation 'ship'. We often pass through a junction where Manny's northern hemisphere winds collide with my southern hemisphere waters. In these moments, the element of air, expressing as analytical male intellect, tries to navigate through my flowing elemental waters of female intuition. It's hard to hide on a yacht; to retreat or become invisible. Sooner or later, everything must be faced and worked with. Sometimes we collaborate, and other times we are polarised like portside and starboard, unable to find midships. In our personal meeting of oceans, we learn to expect anything from broody dark skies that develop into sudden squalls of discord to settled periods of deep love.

Blessed with a rare window of ideal sea and weather conditions, we don't need to make the customary midway rest at the island group of Tuvalu. Our straight nine-day cruise requires minimal sail changes over the entire passage, with the sea so calm that not a drop of dried salt lies on deck. Spectacular electrical storms light up the thundery blue afternoon skies, followed by deluges of rain that come straight down like silver sheets of water. Some days, enough rainwater courses across the decks to wash bedding and towels without using a bucket. How we delight in the luxury of rain showers straight from the heavens above, all the while forging our way across a mighty ocean.

During this glorious ocean crossing, we feel a perfect balance with the ocean, wind, rain, sun, Kaleidoscope, and each other. We could sail forever in utter contentment. We shudder to think about the shock of immigration formalities, the noise of humanity, and the jarring sensations of land after such tranquillity. Stepping through an invisible portal, we enter a timeless zone with an altered reality — a different dimension. But beneath these idyllic calm waters, the dark undercurrent of resentment continues to run its course.

On deck, our single problem is a large white sea bird determined to use the top spreaders of our main mast as a resting place. "Grab the pots and pans," yells Manny, already shooing and shouting.

"Poor thing, it must be exhausted. Nowhere to land for hundreds of miles," I sympathise, craning my neck to see.

"I feel sorry for it too. But navigation and communication equipment are up there. We can't risk it."

We admire its determined attempts at landing on a shifting target, circling again and again, gauging the exact moment to swoop onto the teasing mast. Each evening for the next few days, we stand with reluctance on deck, clanging pots and lids to discourage our unwelcome guest.

The bird's arrival makes me think about spirit guides who use birds as messengers, and I think of Tim and the white owl. By clinging to my old roles of obligation, am I also trying to perch on targets that must move and sway with the necessity of change? As hard as I try to stand on a target that moves and sways with life's natural flow, my attempts prove futile and exhausting, like the poor sea bird circling and circling. What am I missing?

After a night spent tossing and turning on emotional seas, I'm glad to see daylight filtering through the stern portal. I find Manny already on deck with a grin on his face. "Look at this, Sweetie Mouzee," he says, handing me the binoculars.

"Am I seeing things? It looks like a miniature hedge growing in the middle of the ocean."

He chuckles. "That's Kiribati. Your hedge is most likely coconut palms."

"But there're no cliffs, rugged coastline. Nothing," I say, pressing the lens closer."

"Yah. Just one metre above sea level. No mountains like Germany or New Zealand. Help me take down some sail, sweetie, we don't want to approach Tarawa in the dark."

It's still some hours before dawn when we see the outline of tall palms and lights sprinkled here and there around the atoll. It's too risky to go further and we drop anchor in the shallow outer harbour, stationary for the first time in ten days. Without a breeze to counter the oppressive humidity, I jump in the sea to cool down, but it feels like warm soup, thick with salt. Breakfasted and ready at first light, we pull up the anchor and cautiously motor towards the wharf, seeing people hitch up their clothes and wade into the sea for their morning ablutions. Sadly, we would learn that Tarawa's reputation as a Pacific slum was accurate, and limited sewerage system and unclean water meant sixty percent of the population were infected with hepatitis.

Stretching over the bow rail as far as I can without losing my balance, I hear a stream of warning beeps coming from the depth sounder. The noses of semi-submerged fighter planes lie just under the surface, rusted relics the remnants of WWII when America and Japan strategically used Kiribati. It's difficult to imagine the roar of planes coming and going from this remote scrap of land.

Ashore, my senses struggle under an assault of blaring music on a jolting bus ride, and hots clouds of dust rise, choking me in the streets of Tarawa. Roaming cats and dogs poke through coconut shells strewn outside doorways of ramshackle huts. We face this for three days each time we attempt to complete custom formalities. Sometimes we find the right staff member, sweltering in a white shirt and bright tie, but not in possession of the correct rubber stamp. Another time all the necessary papers and stamps are present, but not the official. It's a relief when all factors come together, and we can leave for the outlying atoll of Butaritari with its promising reputation as the 'Garden Island'. With greater rainfall.it sounds the ideal place to top up the water tank and our supplies of fresh produce after our long passage.

Manny soon rigs an efficient water-catching arrangement that doubles as a sunshade and protects our feet from scorching hot decks. The ocean surrounding beautiful Butaritari provides crystal clear waters, and our neighbour is a large American yacht owned by a female skipper. I feel a bit sorry for her young, volunteer crew members who have come alongside in their outboard several times to groan about the unimaginative food onboard their vessel.

We discover the locals don't care for pumpkins, grapefruit, and lemons that would add variety to their staples of pawpaw and coconut, and, like the American skipper, prefer tinned corned beef to plentiful reef fish. Other surprises lie in store as we gather football-sized grapefruit from wild gardens, sometimes coming across open-air thatched huts perched on pole platforms. Hearing the moans of a couple making love we scramble to change direction but are noticed before we can scuttle. Hastily straightening their sarongs they call out waving, insisting we join them for a cup of tea. Sitting with our new friends sharing their afterglow and large aluminium teapot, I notice a bright green gecko peek out of the spout. It retreats for a few moments before popping its comical head out again. An unsettling thought comes to me. Will I have to leave the teapot when the water gets too hot?

Sunday church is a social highlight we can't escape after the local pastor invites us to attend, smiling through gums and teeth stained red from chewing betel quid.

Unused to sitting cross-legged on the floor, Manny and I lean against the back wall of the wooden hall, fascinated as family groups arrive with each shirt or dress brighter and whiter than the next. Sitting close together in rows, thick, glossy black braids escape from beneath the women's straw hats down to their waists, their plump bottoms making a curvaceous line of alphabet 'double-you's.'

The villagers chat throughout the service, coconut hair combs rake through long tresses and skinny dogs wander around. Their big hearts explode into song with each psalm; church is a hot, noisy affair. As soon as the preacher closes the service, the entire congregation bolt like children, trying to squeeze through the door at the same time.

Because of the sweltering heat I light the gas oven or hobs before 6am, and early one morning make two hearty loaves of bread. After using an electric grinder to grind spelt wheat grains into fresh flour the delicious smell of baking bread wafts through Kaleidoscope.

"Mmmm, they smell so good, Sweetie Mouzee," says Manny, drawing the fragrance into his nostrils.

"I'm going to give one to our neighbours."

"Why? We need the bread ourselves."

"They don't have good provisions on board. You've heard them complain when they stop by."

"That's not our concern. We need it."

"But we have heaps of grain. I can bake more." I reason.

"No, Sweetie Mouzee. That's not the point. And you don't need their approval."

My undercurrent of resentment suddenly rears its head and I shout, "What? Then I'll throw both bloody loaves over the side!"

Cut to the bone with this conflict, I find a shady nook on deck as far away from Manny as possible to lick my wounds. I know he's right. My desire to please others is driven by my need to gain their approval. It's just another self-imposed task that stems from my deep-rooted sense of worthlessness. These long-held core beliefs defining who I am all hinged upon a rusty doorframe lacking self-love. When Manny refuses to allow these old roles to play out, I interpret his response as unloving. When in fact, he is doing a masterful job of pulling out deeply embedded beliefs and behaviours, pulling one rusty nail out at a time. It is painful at the time of extraction, and I am far from gracious about it.

It's not just one way. I'm pushing Manny's buttons too. Nothing remains hidden for long on a yacht and by the time we arrived in the Marshall Islands tensions are running high. We have both shut our emotions down and it's clear we can't be on the boat together in this unbearable silence. Fulfilling Manny's fears that I will leave again, I shoulder my backpack and head for the airport, feeling a complicated mix of emotions. I'm relieved to escape the terrible tension, and to know I can now support Laura, but I'm gutted at the cost. Why am I torn between the two people I love? Why is it necessary to rock the boat in this way?

Again, I think about the sea bird who wants to nest on the mast that is constantly shifting beneath it.

Chapter 10

SURRENDER

*'Retracting my lioness claws allows a new perspective.
I see how each time I worry about Laura and run to her rescue,
I invalidate her ability to trust her decisions — her main
lesson for this lifetime.'*

Laura looks radiant. Now a young woman, her strawberry blonde hair and smooth skin glow with vitality. To see her brown eyes shine with excitement instead of tears gladdens my heart. I feel the roundness of her belly as I hug her yet again, making my spirits soar.

"Oh, it moved," I squeal, her stomach pulsing against mine.

"Already knows grandma is here," smiles Laura. "It's good to have you back, Mumsy."

"It's good to have *you* back, darling."

She looks away for a moment. "That's behind me now. I'll never touch another drug."

"I couldn't reach you. You were somewhere else. I went somewhere else too."

She jokes, "Yeah, when people ask me how we coped in the beginning, I say that I took every drug under the sun and Mum went sailing." She adds, "Some people criticised you for not being around. But I always defended you. I knew that you needed to do that."

Wiping a tear, I reply, "You are wise beyond your years, darling. And I'm so grateful you never held me back. I did feel guilty at times."

"You shouldn't. I needed to do what I needed to do. By myself."

"Do you remember Raman saying you would develop great strength? I see this in you, sweetheart." I pause, shepherding a scattering of insight into words. "And I see now how this relates to the way you once reeled Tim back in each time he ventured away. You have allowed a loved one freedom. Thank you for that, darling. I'm so proud of you."

"I'm glad you are my mother."

"Thank you, sweetheart. And I know you will make an amazing mother. Now go and rest."

Provided I don't voice concerns about Jase, we enjoy preparing for the arrival of her new baby. Although Jason isn't working, I find him impossible to talk with. He is either already in bed or disappears out the door the minute I arrive. I can't say I blame him. No doubt he sees me waving my silent flag of disapproval in his face. If only he'd give me some sign of acknowledging his responsibilities, something to help me trust and develop confidence in him.

In the absence of his support for Laura, I attempt to fill that void with good grace. But on the day of the birth, my anger at Jase rears up, triggered by his swagger.

Catching sight of his lean frame leaving the maternity ward, I corner him.

"Why don't you clear out?" I snarl. "You've done nothing to help. Laura and I can raise this baby." This fierce side of me surprises him. The lioness protecting her cubs.

"You can't talk to me like that," he stammers, taken aback.

My heart hammers in my chest. "Just fuck off! Leave us alone." He turns and leaves, with me glowering at his long back.

Laura dissolves, devastated at my actions. "That's all I need. You two fighting. You know Tim wanted us all to get along."

I hang my head in shame. To his credit, Jason does attempt to get his act together. He tries various jobs, succeeding in the beginning. But, full of pain and anger at life, he falls back to his default position of victim. Sooner or later, he feels unjustly treated by a colleague or management and quits. Laura separates from him at times but returns each time, and I am forced to accept the strong magnetic pull between them. Like Manny and me.

Aarliah Rose brings our family much joy. My jar of balm, she softens the hard edges around my heart. Laura amplifies her natural ability to nurture, demonstrated since she was a young girl caring for animals. Unlike me, she takes to motherhood like a duck to water. As though her bottomless love for her brother resides inside a deep well, now she draws it up in bucketfuls.

Retracting my lioness claws allows a new perspective. I see that each time I worry about Laura and run to her rescue, I invalidate her ability to trust her decisions. The very thing she needs to learn in this lifetime. Worse, I recognise that my insecurity, based around feeling needed and worthy of love, drives my meddling. I don't need to save anybody. I don't need to please everybody. I don't need to bake bloody loaves of bread for strangers. Manny was trying to tell me I'm good enough!

This shocking self-revelation comes to me while sitting with little Aarliah Rose asleep in my arms. Ashamed, I revisit my reaction to the news of her impending arrival. I determine to release this wound of unworthiness and sit behind the driving wheel. The adorable bundle of warmth nestled against my chest shifts her weight, synchronised with my shifting perspective. At peace with myself, I trace a finger over her soft rosy cheeks, bend my head, and kiss the crown of her head.

"Have you landed here before?" inquires the American man seated next to me.

"No, I haven't. Last time I arrived by boat. Over a year ago. A hair-raising experience, I can tell you. All those plane wrecks in the water."

"Yeah," he muses through raised eyebrows. "Well, let me tell you something. Brace yourself."

Arrival in Tarawa by air frightens the hell out of me. The entire length of the runway stretches from one side of the tiny atoll to the other. Even forewarned, my knuckles grow white gripping the armrest as we head straight towards the ocean. At least I don't scream.

Manny stands at the edge of the tarmac. Delighted about our reunion, he's sailed from the Marshall Islands back to Tarawa in time to meet my flight. I feel so happy with his arms around me, and we chat while airport staff unload the luggage.

"You look good, Sweetie Mouzee."

"So do you. You feel different."

"Oh?" he smiles. "I am different. I have learned a lot about myself."

"Me too. I can't wait to see Kaleidoscope."

"Yah, let's have a rum."

Fijian baggage handlers haven't reloaded my backpack at the Nandi stopover, leaving me stranded with just the contents of my handbag. For three days of suffocating heat, I wear a small blue gingham tablecloth as a sarong. We set sail for Vanuatu the moment my luggage turns up.

The dynamics of our relationship feel renewed. Without realising it, we had both planted our fear of loss in our garden. True to the laws of nature, it had flowered in exact accordance with the seeds sown. Now, having weeded out those noxious plants, a refreshing level of authenticity can germinate.

Sitting on deck in my mini sarong, watching the sun go down, I turn to Manny, "You know, I feel like I'm getting to know who I really am."

He winks. "The real you is definitely showing, Sweetie Mouzee."

I tug at my sarong with a laugh. "Maybe that's why my old clothes didn't arrive on the plane."

"Ha," he chuckles. "You are right. New clothes for the new you."

"It's amazing how what happens on the inside turns up on the outside," I muse. "Now, tell me more about that Marshall Island story. The one about the raft."

He nods, looking satisfied. "A good project. It has been a long time since anyone built a new raft there. Their fishing grounds are depleted, and the men of that village were quite down, depressed."

"You stayed some time with them?"

"Yes, it worked better that way. Too dangerous to navigate on my own. So, I stayed a long time in each place. I spent a lot of my time reflecting. I missed you, Sweetie Mouzee."

Our genuine devotion and respect for each other once again transcend our travails. Grateful to be together again, an extra tenderness marks this next phase of our union. We have both learned a valuable lesson about holding resentment, having seen how fast it had spread through our relationship. Excited, we map out our next five months in Vanuatu before heading back to New Zealand. Thanks to Manny's knowledge of weather systems, we enjoy another magical ten-day passage, and thanks to our inner work, emotional barometers remain stable.

We make landfall in the Banks Islands, a place seldom visited by yachts and the villagers on this remote group of islands at Vanuatu's farthest-flung tip are eager to interact with us. Lots of hand-flapping and expressive faces convey our thoughts, except to the customs official who we couldn't track down. Low on perishable goods, we trade salt for fresh vegetables and fruit. Manny finds himself in demand for repairing mechanical items. The clocks that nobody takes any notice of, and an antiquated but well-utilised treadle sewing machine are infested with the cause of their failure, colonies of cockroaches.

My legendary Banks Islands coconut cake doesn't involve evicting squatters, thank goodness. Adapting a recipe to locally grown foods, except flour which the makeshift shop provides, we measure cups of freshly grated coconut and squeezed coconut cream, cane sugar, and vanilla beans straight from pods. The village women take charge of the next stage, steaming the cake inside a tin 'billy' over a wood fire. No comparison can be made between desiccated coconut and canned coconut cream, and the mouthwatering cake is an instant hit.

All Vanuatu children celebrate their birthdays on the same day, a practical solution to redundant calendars and clocks. The new recipe coincides with this annual event, each family making a cake and gathering for an afternoon of games and music. A local string band plays a vigorous kind of swing music on their homemade instruments, yet no one twirls to their joyful plucking sounds.

"Do you dance?" I ask a new friend sitting next to me under a tree, her hands folded in her lap.

"No," she says, shaking her head. "It's not Christian."

Strong trade winds arrive to take us further south to the mainland. We anchor in the clear, sheltered waters of Big Bay on the northeastern coast of Vanuatu's largest island, Espiritu Santo. This area contains many wonderful species of trees and birds and boasts the recent claim of home to the country's first national park.

Big Bay provides an idyllic anchorage and, during the next six weeks, we make many friends in the village. With more exposure to cruisers and the magic of soap powder already reaching Big Bay, the women accept my washing ways in the freshwater stream. I dry my washing onboard, but they spread their clothes over the sand, placing small rocks to prevent items from blowing away. Looking down on this scene from a nearby hilltop, it resembles a massive quilt in the making.

Years earlier, missionaries had taught Chief Solomon and his wife, Purity, Pidgin English, enabling this delightful couple to promote the nation's first national park. They are keen to recruit our assistance in creating an advertising brochure, and Manny takes many wonderful photographs for them. One evening, excitement ripples through the village in anticipation of movie night, a showing of forest and village photos on our laptop. Familiar trees and flowering plants are recognised, despite their Lilliputian scale. But Manny had also taken close-up shots of a small tree spider, captivated by its exotic patterns. When it filled the entire computer screen, the kids scream with fright and run away. Most of the adults jump too.

Unaccustomed to seeing themselves this way, the villagers break into fits of giggles. Mirrors are a scarcity and they lean forward to inspect their image on the screen with delightful shyness. Several comment they hadn't appreciated the beauty of their village until captured by the camera. Most of our new friends bear names from the Old Testament but during our stay some young parents name their newborn after 'Manny'!

Purity remarks, "It's good to introduce a new name in the village."

While in Big Bay, Manny and I receive many opportunities to practice living in the present moment. Unlike people in so-called developed countries, units of time are held in low regard by the islanders.

"How long does it take to get to the next village?" I check with Solomon one day. He stares at me without answering.

"Is it far?" I encourage. "An hour's walk?"

"Yes," he smiles, showing yellow teeth. "One hour."

Anything relating to time constitutes an ineffective question to ask an islander. In their down-to-earth practical experience, you are either here, or you are there. And you will know when you are there because you are not here anymore. Between here and there is up to you. Therefore, how can they predict a journey?

However, knowing time is important to their visitors, they do their best to help. Manny and I need to travel to Luganville at the southernmost tip of Santo to complete immigration formalities. Thanks to the elusive official in the Banks Islands, we lack visas. Solomon suggests we speak to Chief Peter, who transports fish from Big Bay to Luganville most days. Our arrangement to travel with him the next day includes the unusual request to be ready at the specific time of 9 a.m. We arrive on time the next morning, then twiddle our thumbs for an hour before we find our driver.

"I'm not going today. No fish. Come back tomorrow," he grins, with no sense of needing to apologise.

We repeat this three mornings running until we are underway in the back of his truck, bouncing along with boxes of fish and sacks of copra. After the two-hour bone-shattering drive, two hours remain to clear customs and find provisions. Chief Peter says to be ready at 3 p.m.

Darkness approaches with the setting sun. A helpful passerby points to a grassy area across the road, saying, "That's where people sleep when they can't get back to Big Bay." Manny and I exchange glances but feel sure Chief Peter will arrive. Two hours later, he pulls up, full of apologies for his lateness due to mechanical problems. Neither Manny nor I display anger as we heave provisions into the back. "Must have been big cockroaches under the bonnet," I joke.

"Yah," agrees Manny, "Expect the unexpected."

Without warning, the wind changes direction one day, placing Kaleidoscope at risk. Lucky to be onboard, we rush to dismantle the washing line, stow the shade covers, and make the galley safe. We hope our special friends understand why we can't go ashore and say our goodbyes.

Again, we venture further south, heading for a sheltered anchorage popular with yachties on the island of Malekula. Within a few hours of arriving, Chief Willie and his sister paddle over in an outrigger canoe and welcome us to their village. Accustomed to visiting yachts, Chief Willie speaks Pidgin English through yellowish tusk-like teeth protruding from his long, thin face. After exchanging the usual information about our families and learning about my two children, an unexpected conversation follows.

"Two childs?" he questions, holding up two grubby fingers.

I nod and smile.

He counts on nine fingers and says, "My wife has dis babies. You have two? You have da liddle pills?"

Recovering from this surprise and not at all sure where this is leading, I lie. In truth, I use an IUD, but I doubt pidgin English or propriety will take us there.

His face brightens. "Do you have some for my wife? The nurse doesn't come now. With da liddle pills. No more babies. No more."

Oh no! My small lie forces me to cover it with a bigger one. Manny's eyes twinkle with amusement, but he manages to keep a straight face. I explain as best as I can that the pills are all different, and my pills might not be safe for his wife. Thankfully, he accepts my explanation and the subject changes.

Chief Willie's shy, younger sister stays silent during the conversation. Noticing she often looks at my feet, I fetch the bottle and paint her toenails the same colour as mine.

SURRENDER

She looks pleased when I offer her the bottle plus a bright lipstick that suits her dark skin. Chief Willie, intrigued by these feminine tools, snatches the lipstick from his sister and smears it over his generous lips. The situation calls for more straight faces.

The next day, every man, woman and child we meet sports one painted fingernail, but there's no sign of lipstick. Perhaps Chief Willie keeps it for his wife. Premature aging of Vanuatu women from their physical labour of growing food in the sun and birthing many babies is their norm.

The naturalness of living in a timeless zone with our intimate connection to each other and Mother Nature brings deep satisfaction. Discovering new friends and different perspectives keeps us sailing from one exotic destination to the next. Yet we also value the freedom to retreat from the rest of the world into our self-sufficient paradise if we choose to. During those precious times, listening to our favourite music, reading books, and continual debating fill our minds and hearts. Sipping a sundowner on deck, watching the sun slip from sight, I carry enormous gratitude for my life. It exceeds the dreams I'd written as little notes to the universe and tucked inside the pocket of Tim's work belt. Sometimes I even hold Tim in my heart without crying.

Nearing the end of our five-month stay in Vanuatu, we arrive at the cruiser's dream anchorage of Lamens Bay, Epi Island. Home to the dugong (sea cow), although it normally feeds on sea lettuce that grows on the ocean floor, we often hear one nibbling away just under our hull. I love to jump in the water and watch this curious creature whose body resembles a seal with a cow's head. There's something humble about this placid animal. We often watch cavorting dolphins and large turtles swimming around Kaleidoscope too.

Beachcombing reveals beautiful shells, and the villagers supply fresh vegetables, fruits, and clean water aplenty. Local residents invite the lively exchange of conversations and ideas brought to their doorsteps by cruisers from around the world. Their charming island sits a one-day sail from Port Vila, the capital, from where most cruisers arrive and depart.

One family grows succulent eggplants from gifted seeds but is unsure how to use them. Manny and I demonstrate diverse ways of cooking the glossy purple and white vegetables, mastering a battered fry pan over a smoky fire. It amazes me how adults never worry about infants toddling around with a large knife in their hands. Burning and slashing create communal gardens, and I seldom see a villager without a machete. I watch, fascinated, as a man using a huge, clumsy knife finely dices spring onions in the open palm of his hand.

In this harmonious, idyllic setting, I reflect on the slashing and burning of my inner garden. Following this line of insight, I walk through rows of newly planted self-beliefs, noting little green shoots breaking through the hard soil. I wander around the older, established part of my garden looking for Corky. Pulling back thick vines, I gasp at this thorny, entangled part of the garden. Corky isn't there, and I look again in my new garden. She isn't there either. A low-seated panic slithers around my belly.

Chapter 11

DARK NIGHT OF THE SOUL

*'For the first time in my life, I feel empty.
Exposed, with not even a small, blue gingham tablecloth
to hide behind.'*

Over the ensuing days, disturbing thoughts stalk the edges of my mind. Like a panther prowling the perimeter of a watering hole, waiting to pounce on the unguarded.

Deep down, I know I live behind a frontage masking the real me. And going even deeper, I sense another version of me, an authentic me, on the other side of this façade. Leaning against the wall, I try to visualise her. Perhaps this woman resembles the beautiful, unpretentious people of the Pacific Islands that I admire. Their simple, honest ways magnify the complexities and falsehoods built around me like a medieval walled city.

Amid the confusion, one thing becomes crystal clear — Corky has jumped overboard. Only her thin trail of wake remains in the water as she distances herself from me. I run in panic to untie the rope and throw her a lifeline… but I freeze at the handrails, gasp, and let her go.

I no longer recognise the empty woman looking out to sea. Desperate, I cast about for her identity, even pathetically calling out to Annette. With horror, I remember I've sent her packing, along with her bags of grief. I forced her to walk the plank!

Turning my head in all directions, looking under every coil of rope, I search for her. Perhaps she has survived, somehow. I spy white knuckles gripping the end of the plank and with effort, haul her shrivelled form back on board. She still wears her soggy sack of sorrow tied around her neck. I stare at her, incredulous at her tenacity. She isn't how I remember her at all but, at that moment, she is all I have.

Annette grips my wrist and yanks me straight back into her core beliefs. She watched Corky jump. No longer diminished, she swells up with importance, flooding my bilges with wretched thoughts. My hard-won, consciously retrained beliefs unravel like a dropped bobbin. I watch them gurgle and slither out the boat's drainage holes.

Self-admonishing thoughts take hold. Laura's struggles, and my former voluntary community work haunt me. Once again, I bear accountability for former pupils and remember my constant availability for friends. How could I leave them all? When did I turn into this self-centred creature sailing around the Pacific Islands, living a privileged lifestyle when others need me? Even my daughter.

Devastated, I fall back to my default position, projecting my inner turmoil towards Manny. How dare he deprive me of my family, my friends, my community, my country! Bewildered at this huge emotional swing after our peaceful travels together, I can't make sense of it. Logic, reason, and truth lie far in the distance.

None of my misgivings are voiced aloud, but my body eavesdrops, absorbing every vulnerable thought and emotion. Feeling sullen while winching in a sail on our way to Port Vila, a searing pain tears across my lower back. For three days, I can't roll over, sit up, or walk. Manny does everything for me. Using his height and strength, he drags me to the heads, my feet trailing on the floor, with my arms wrapped around his neck. I cry out in agony as the erratic motion of the boat creates more pain. At his wit's end, Manny radios a German doctor who suggests exercises and medications from our supplies.

Feeling miserable, angry, and resentful at being dependent on Manny, I silently pray to be off the yacht. As soon as possible. No other choice remains but to surrender. But to what?

We make fast time to Port Vila in the strong coastal winds. Immigration formalities complete, we wait for our window to New Caledonia. Proper rest in a calm anchorage makes an enormous difference to my recovery, each day regaining movement in my legs, but I still hobble about.

Although Manny understands I'm struggling with something, he can't know the extent of my epic internal storm. Sensitive to my painful body, he holds back an unsettling weather report for as long as he can.

"Sweetie Mouzee, I don't want to alarm you, but a weather fax arrived issuing a warning. There's an early cyclone approaching."

"Oh, hell. What are the chances?"

"It's headed straight for Port Vila. Don't worry. We're safe here."

"What do we need to do?" I ask, acutely aware of my impaired mobility.

"I can do it, Sweetie. Just rest. I'll clear everything off the deck."

"I'll stow everything below deck."

"Do what you can, Sweetie Mouzee, no more. The mainsail must be roped to the mast. You might have to help me with that. And I'll hire a diver to check our mooring and set an extra anchor. That's all we can do."

The news sends all the cruisers into a frenzied haste to clear the decks of their vessels and stow everything as securely as possible. We watch the local ferries coax their vessels bow-first onto the beach of the small island in front of which we are all sheltering. They lash the vessels with heavy ropes to trees, and then the ferries are roped to each other.

Along Vanuatu coastlines, villagers light massive bonfires to ward off the spirits of the dreaded winds. Manny and I agree we'll remain on Kaleidoscope unless it becomes unsafe. The prospect of climbing into the dinghy, bucking in screaming winds, further strains my frayed nerves. Right now, I doubt I could manage even in calm conditions. An uncustomary quiet descends over the full anchorage and marina, with cruisers staying below deck tracking the cyclone on their computers. We hold our breath along with the others.

Night falls, adding another layer of anxiety. Clearing the decks, stowing below, and tightening ropes somehow parody my internal process.

Around midnight an updated weather fax arrives, and a cheer bounces around the boats. The cyclone has veered away from Port Vila at the last moment. Spontaneous parties and the merry clinking of glasses replace the anxious wait, relief flowing with the outpouring of beer until the small hours of the morning.

After waiting three days for calmer seas, we sail the three-day route to New Caledonia, where a French chiropractor eases my back pain enough to endure the rigors of the final passage back to New Zealand. Manny takes extra care and picks the best weather window of the season. Our comfortable six-day sail contrasts with others who left a few days earlier and battled stormy conditions on their way back. Some ended up closer to Australia than New Zealand.

I heave an enormous sigh of relief when the familiar sight of Sail Rock comes into view, announcing we are home. Manny turns Kaleidoscope starboard to make our way into the calm waters of the beautiful Bay of Islands. The moment customs officers leave, without a word, I pack my meagre belongings into my backpack. The tension of the cyclone, sailing an ocean passage with an injured back, and months of deep processing have left me utterly spent. With an overwhelmed nervous system, it takes focus to place one foot in front of the other. Carrying mental, emotional, and physical exhaustion to an even greater degree than after Tim died, I am on the verge of collapse. And desperate to be alone.

"When will you be back, Sweetie Mouzee?" Manny asks in a low, soft voice.

Through blurred tears, I slur the few words I can muster, "I don't know, darling. I don't know the answer to that. I can't think. Can't find words. I'm sorry."

As I hug Manny goodbye, although tears stream down my face, I detect no real emotion. For the first time in my life, I feel empty. Exposed, with not even a small, blue gingham tablecloth to hide behind.

Chapter 12

BABUSHKA DOLL

*'Believing myself healed from grief,
I've reinvented myself as Corky.'*

Christchurch gardens are in full bloom at their summer peak while I'm slumped in an all-time low. A row of clipped cypress trees directs my gaze above rooftops, over to Diamond Harbour opposite Lyttelton. From the dormer window, I gaze down at the formal Italian garden, complete with a circular rose bed and an impressive water fountain. Inhaling the sweet scent of freshly picked Peace roses, I yearn for their promised tranquillity. Six years since Tim transitioned back to Spirit, I'm finally face to face with my self-deception. I can no longer ignore the gaping hole in my heart, and now I hold fresh grief for Manny. We will never find our way back together from here. I've left too many times.

Manny had seen right through my Corky character and dared me to throw away the script. He'd found all my stashed provisions and joggled those mental constructs out of their hiding place, one by one. Exposed, raw, and vulnerable, I needed a safe retreat. Somewhere, anywhere, where a small sack of pain wouldn't be noticed. Convinced the solution lay in returning to my familiar shore-based life, I resumed my old roles. Surely, I would find myself here again?

Hearing Laura downstairs chatting with my hosts, Lea and Pav, I brush away my tears. By the time she coaxes Aarliah Rose to toddle up the steep, narrow, creaky stairs of the former Anglican vicarage, I'm wearing my brave face.

"It's great having you back in Christchurch, Mumsy. Do you have your land legs yet?"

"Not really, sweetie. I feel like a duck out of water."

"No wonder. You've lived on the water so long. Do you miss Manny?"

I nod. "But I love spending time with you and Aarliah Rose. And it's wonderful to walk the peninsula hills again."

"And talk to your trees, you old hippie," she teases. It's a habit I've had since childhood.

"At least they don't give me any lip." I laugh. "By the way, I plan to put an ad in the paper. I'm thinking of working as a live-in help for a senior person or something like that. I visualise an old character house with a rambling garden."

"Great idea!" she enthuses. "Somewhere to live, plus income."

In truth, I lack her enthusiasm. But while scanning the newspaper ads to see what format to use, an interesting position catches my eye. The exclusive and private Rangi Ruru School, with an overflow of students in their main boarding house this year, needs a housemother. The successful applicant will live in a charming character house set in their park-like grounds and supervise a small group of adolescent girls. Goodbye zimmer frame, I think, and hello iPods.

My return ashore to the 'Garden City of Christchurch' lands me right in the nursery beds of social conditioning. Employed to cultivate the same core beliefs I've weeded out, the irony isn't lost on me. Within a week, I've settled into a tree-lined suburb near Hagley Park and Avon River walks. Lea and Pav loan antique beds and sofas to furnish my elegant rooms, and I revel in the spaciousness and privacy.

The six girls leave the house at 8 am each morning, leaving me free to tutor private students during the day. It also allows precious time with my adorable little granddaughter and, after several trips to the river with a bag of breadcrumbs, Aarliah Rose says her first word, 'duck'.

Dropping Arli off one morning, Laura asks how things are going.

"Well, it couldn't be more different from living aboard with Manny," I say, rolling my eyes. "There's heavy social conditioning going on here, I tell you. It's no wonder humans lose their authentic selves."

"I wouldn't like to look after fifteen-year-olds. I remember what I was like," she grins. "Are boys allowed?"

"God, no. But when I flipped a blue cotton sheet onto a bed for the first group, I saw a written message that hadn't washed out. Someone's delightful daughter used a vivid black marker to draw an arrow outside a small circle. The message by the arrow said, "Matthew came here. It was lovely.""

Laura roars with laughter. "Oh Mum, that's so funny. Do they behave for you?"

"It's interesting because compared to the main boarding house, they have a lot more freedom here. They're used to fighting for freedom by challenging petty authority, but they haven't figured out that there's no one to lock horns with. They look confused when I ignore their little games."

With each passing month, I settle back into life ashore. Returning to the familiar helps me navigate the dark void of the unknown that yawns before me. But that shocking rawness begins to ease, thanks to a new friend and her timely book. Marti and I became friends during a recent training course, updating our teaching skills to assist children with learning difficulties. Like me, Marti possesses a playful quality — Manny would have described her as flirtatious. Her blue eyes twinkle past her thick mascara and oversized framed glasses, yet she also knows loss.

I'm still devouring her loaned copy of 'The Power of Now' by Eckhart Tolle.

Taking care to set my cup on the coaster protecting her polished walnut coffee table, I say, "God, Marti, we've just met, and yet I have so much to thank you for. Tolle gives me such hope. He describes exactly what I went through.

"Ah," she says, "You reminded me of having to leave my farm and family in South Africa. I recognised your struggle of leaving an old life behind before the new arrives… and the incredible insecurity that brings."

My shoulders drop and I sigh, the feelings of anguish still fresh.

"Yeah, that's the toughest part. Straddling both old and new. Not knowing where to put my feet. I realised I had lived my life through others, instead of claiming my own place in the world. An astonishing revelation. It gives me comfort to know others go through this. And that it's not for nothing."

She leans forward and tops up my tea, her face soft with compassion. "Go on."

"You might find the pages of your book stuck together," I joke. "I cried with sheer relief knowing I wasn't going insane. I felt Tolle rise off the pages and reach into my mind. He's so bloody honest about his own experience." I stop and shake my head. Never before has a book impacted me in that way. "As though his words took me by the scruff of my neck and pulled me back from the edge of a dark pit. One hard to climb out of."

Marti agrees. "You can see why it's called the 'dark night of the soul.' Are you feeling more at peace now?"

"Some moments of peace. And I'm gentle with myself," I say, my mouth trembling as I confide, "But I feel such sorrow, Marti. It's like a new abyss of grief has opened. I thought I'd healed from grief. All I did was reinvent myself as Corky. Then I realised, although I've healed many beliefs, my heart still aches." Warm tears wet my cheeks, and my voice becomes small. "I haven't been able to connect with Tim for ages."

In her wise, warm voice, she says, "Well, perhaps you're ready to do that piece of work now. Now you've released so many old beliefs, you're open to other things. I know you'll find your beautiful boy again."

"I hope so, Marti."

She hesitates, "What about Manny? Should I ask? I don't wish to pry."

Managing a weak smile, "No, not at all. It's good to have a friend to share with." I draw a breath and finger the pendant around my neck that he gave to me. "I miss him."

That night, after yelling 'lights out' to the giggling girls upstairs, I return to the book that brings comforting insights. Fascinated by the 'dark night of the soul,' I wonder why no one talks about this. Everybody must experience it at some point in their lives. Is it just us New Zealanders, proud of our number eight fencing wire resilience, who haven't heard of it? Or is it denial?

Tolle describes how, at first, he struggles to release ego-driven roles — what I call core beliefs. He writes that each time we cast off yet another outdated core belief, our ego feels diminished. Desperate to reclaim power once more, it fights back. Tolle calls this scenario 'automatic ego-repair mechanisms'. Poor Manny stood in the firing line each time my ego tried to restore itself using self-justification, defence, and blame. It seems the ego is more interested in self-preservation than truth.

Now, I'm at a fragile but pivotal point in my journey. Will I surrender to governance by my ego-driven reality, or will I take a leap of faith into a new, unknown reality? I think of the false bricks Manny dismantled from my façade, allowing me to glimpse my true self. Squinting through this gap, I fall asleep.

Tolle's book still lay on my chest when I woke late the next morning to the girls' black lace-ups tramping down the stairway. The smell of burnt toast and sound of shrieking chatter assaulted the air until both faded away, leaving the house quiet again. In a moment of rare indulgence, I shed my dressing gown and returned to bed. In a peaceful doze, halfway between worlds, unspoken words satiated my ears.

"Greetings beloved. I am Centatron, one of your guides. I am here to affirm the process through which you have journeyed, and to celebrate this inner work. As you released many of your erroneous beliefs, you moved through a transition stage. You felt deep vulnerability while in that unknown phase. Layers and layers of altered-ego have lifted off - rather like the layers of the Russian Babushka doll. The most difficult aspect of that stage lay with your temporary lack of tools with which to rebuild your new self."

Lying stock still, waiting for more words, the message ended. This heartwarming confirmation, and the nature of its delivery, raised up my spirits. Relating to the metaphoric Babushka doll, I indeed recalled how my diminished ego reared up and roared with vengeance, desperate to return as Annette. In this light, I perceived my ego as a wobbly, wooden doll with a painted face, feeling its own fragility. In a flash of clarity I understood its need to be loved, without allowing it to grab the driving wheel.

'A temporary lack of tools,' Centatron said. So true. Set adrift in a rudderless vessel, impossible to follow the stars without knowing where true north lay. Until, no longer tenable, there remained no other choice but to jump ship without the security of landfall. The leap of faith.

I now viewed the traditional boarding school as excellent testing ground. I accepted a private challenge to inwardly resist succumbing to the pressure of doing things the way things were always done. Continuing in a world shaped by conditioned thoughts and behaviours would no longer do. It became essential to walk between worlds while rebuilding my Babushka doll with authentic layers. I was in the boarding school but not of it.

Tolle's information facilitated a rapid shift in my reality. My determination to follow through with his wisdom soon replaced despair with excitement. Pretending a wise old owl perched on my shoulder, I self-queried my thoughts and critiqued my words. Were they my own inner thoughts and words, or did they belong to my mother, my teacher, my partner? Within a few weeks this exercise of discernment became automatic, allowing me to observe roles played by others. Their pretences were now so obvious I wondered why I'd never noticed before. During this revelatory period, another excitement built - if Centatron could commune with me, perhaps Tim could too.

Eleven months passed since leaving Manny, the longest period we'd spent apart. But we continued our contact through emails and I couldn't wait to share Tolle with him. My expanded awareness created extraordinary results, opening the doors to compassion and forgiveness for everything I'd experienced in our unique relationship. Manny also showed a new level of flexibility, suggesting I join him on Kaleidoscope for the New Zealand summer or… for as long as I liked.

Manny waited at the bus stop to greet me. "Sweetie Mouzee! Can I call you that again?" he asked, stooping to kiss me.

"Only you can call me that, sweet man."

We walked down the steep hill to Opua Marina, exchanging our news. Apart from a new pot plant hanging above the dining table, Kaleidoscope looked the same. I stowed my clothes and joined Manny in the cockpit to watch the sun slip between bush-clad hills.

"Do you feel we are still in relationship, Sweetie Mouzee?" asked Manny after downing two rum and cokes.

I felt the wise owl on my shoulder shuffle its feet. My heart stirred, I took a calming breath. "Manny," I softened my voice and swivelled to look at him. "To be honest, I have a sense of completion between us."

To my relief, he relaxed with a smile. "I do, too. That's good. We are agreed. Thank you, Sweetie Mouzee."

"Thank you, Manny. It wasn't easy for you."

"It wasn't easy for you either," he laughed. He cocked his head to one side and said, "Each time we reconnect, we are in a different place with each other."

"Ah huh, that's true. Because we are in a different place within ourselves. Thanks to your fellow countryman, Mr Tolle, I am more toll-er-ant."

"Toll-er-ant… Oh, a corny Christchurch joke. Very good!"

For two months we enjoyed the beauty of our favourite places in the Bay of Islands and Great Barrier Island. As observer of my thoughts, I no longer reacted to situations which in previous times had triggered a defensive response. At times when an old wound resurfaced, a mild degree of irritation briefly replaced my former anger.

Manny returned to the islands the following year and towards the end of the cruising season, suggested I join him to explore New Caledonia. His invitation turned out prophetic because this time Manny injured his back. The same chiropractor in Noumea worked on Manny for a fortnight while we reversed the roles. Considering his responsibility for the yacht and pride in his physical fitness, Manny held much to surrender, which he did with good grace. With painkillers and care, he was deemed fit for the passage back to New Zealand and I remained onboard until he could manage by himself again.

From the moment of birth, Harlin looked the spitting image of his Uncle Tim. He'd arrived in October 2008 and, unlike Arli, he felt familiar. Laura sensed this too.

"It's his eyes, Mumsy. They're already deep brown like Tim's. Remember Raman said we'd know him by his eyes?"

"I do sweetheart. He does look like Tim as a newborn. Quite different to Arli." Although tempted to go down this track, I held back, recalling another part of Raman's message about Tim's reincarnation.

"You don't think it's him?" Laura tried not to look too hopeful. Harlin nestled in her arms, already at her breast. She gave a gentle tug at his tuft of reddish hair. "He's got the right hair colour. And long legs."

"There is no denying the physical resemblance. But remember, too, that Raman said he would reincarnate into our family, and within a different culture."

"Jase is half Dutch."

"True. But he doesn't live that culture. Let's not get our hopes too high just yet."

"You're right, as usual. It will unfold."

"That's it, wise mother owl," I smiled, lifting the sleeping baby into his bassinette. "He smells divine. Get some sleep darling."

Eight years of extraordinary change and growth were behind me. Six of them spent with what fitted into my backpack. Two years of integration plateaued into a brand-new level of quietude. On the outer, things appeared similar to when Tim died, with family and teaching filled my time. But on the inner, radical change had occurred. Material possessions meant nothing to me. Quite a shift from one who trained and worked as an interior designer prior to teaching. The painted fingernails of Vanuatu villagers taught me how a gift sat in each moment and saw no need to hoard. I teased Lea and Pav whose house bulged with priceless collections they couldn't bear to part with.

Travelling lighter in the world often put me out of step with others. The gap between my conditioned and authentic selves widened, becoming noticeable amongst old friends. They were unsure how to approach this updated version no longer playing her old roles. My changed motives and modus operandi meant I chose to place my energies into sustainable situations. This made them uncomfortable, and although liberated by establishing new, authentic expectations, it proved a lonely period.

With stark clarity, I understood why most of humanity functioned from limited, unconscious beliefs and behaviours. Shaped over thousands of lifetimes on Earth, their acquired mental constructs received continuous endorsement from the collective. With this mental conditioning so deeply embedded in the human psyche, it would take a 'dark night of the soul' to break free from shackles of delusion. Like me, many would resist having someone rifle through and unpack their baggage. Although ungracious at the time, with the wisdom of hindsight, I held profound gratitude for Manny.

Slowly and subtly, loneliness morphed into aloneness, and I relished feeling empowered to be content with my own company. The garish layers of alter-ego were stripped away, my Babushka Doll dismantled and rebuilt. Only authentic choices entered her different layers, and I happily left plenty of empty space for the unknown. This simple, uncluttered life felt natural to me, allowing a deep, inner peace to reside there. Although my doll on occasions wobbled with uncertainty, I understood the underlying promise, that in time, stability and peace would never be dismantled.

Chapter 13

SOUL LESSONS

*'Having away cleared away acquired mental constructs
I began to heal my emotional body, my heart.'*

Two hot topics scorched my list. It had been several years since my last talk with Raman, and although resting against the same overstuffed Indian cushions, I sat in a very different place.

"Salaam dear heart. I am pleased to talk with you again about the things on your mind and in your heart."

"Thank you, Raman. It's good to be here again. I've done so much inner work since Tim returned to Spirit eight years ago." I paused, my voice dropping to a whisper as water pricked my eyes. "But can you explain why I can't connect with him? I thought our communication would get easier over time." I listened without looking up.

"You have indeed done much work, dear heart. Like you, Tim has also been busy, and therefore not as available.

Currently, he is learning about ancient healing under the wings of Archangel Raphael. And he acts a kind of courier, a messenger for the Archangels."

"The Archangels? How very beautiful," I paused to absorb this. "But I still don't understand why I felt so disconnected from him."

"Understand, dear heart, that while you were releasing your erroneous core beliefs, this placed you in a low vibrational frequency. This was unavoidable as conflicted emotions surfaced, and again when you transitioned through the 'dark night of the soul'. This is the stage that humans find difficult. It requires a leap of faith, as you humans call it. It requires trust."

"What do you mean by low vibrational frequencies?"

"Dear heart, our universe is made of energy. Those energies vibrate at different frequencies. In addition, there are Universal Laws, and here we speak of the Law of Attraction. This means it's only possible to connect with energies and frequencies within the same vibrational spectrum. Do you understand, dear heart?"

"I think so. Rather like birds of a feather flock together?"

"From the human perspective that adage refers to humans with similar interests and beliefs. But from the spiritual perspective, it would refer to vibrational frequencies, and is also correct," he smiled, before continuing. "You see, in the physical world, spirits aren't attracted through shared opinions, beliefs and interests. Instead, the attraction occurs through their states of consciousness, which in turn creates their vibrational frequency. For example, for Tim to work alongside archangels, he needed to evolve his consciousness to match theirs. While he experienced joy, bliss, peace and cosmic love, you were in the depths of despair and uncertainty."

A light bulb flicked on. "So, when I match my vibrational frequencies with Tim's, we can commune again?"

"Correct again, dear heart. This is a subject that will become of great interest to you in the coming years."

Reading my thoughts he continued, "And now, I see you have questions about your journey with Manny. I am delighted to share some insights with you, but first I wish to congratulate you both. Because in your six years together, a blink of an eye from our perspective, you completed soul work that would normally take four or five incarnations. You both agreed to fast track this work, because you have other things to attend to in this lifetime. This is why it was intense, at times, for you both."

He waited until I stopped sobbing. His words had spoken to the depths of my soul, and my human side felt a surge of huge relief to understand the soul purpose behind our extraordinary relationship. Raman explained that Manny and I had established a pattern of coming together and moving apart during previous lifetimes. It was the way we chose to work out our soul lessons together. Our long history of deep love and respect for each other compelled us to get back together after each round of taxing trials and tribulations. Dearest Manny, how I loved that man!

There was one particular lifetime set in an English city in the 18th century mentioned by Raman. Manny was my brother, aged about twelve-years-old and I was his eight-year-old sister. We were impoverished orphans forced to beg or scavenge food each day to survive, yet we also created adventures and fun. But tragedy struck when Manny became sick and died. Leaving me grieving and fending for myself, I almost starved to death.

"Like Laura, I too lost my adored brother."

"Indeed. Understand, dear heart, that it was equally important to share happy times together on Kaleidoscope. It was a part of your souls' contract to heal previous experiences of poverty and grief that you and Manny endured together. To enjoy each other in the energies of abundance and joy restored a balance to the energies of your experiences together. This is often called karma, but it is more about balancing vibrational frequencies."

To gain this understanding through the lens of my soul lessons brought tremendous relief and peace. Over the following weeks I contemplated these insights into former lifetimes with Manny, acutely aware of the abandonment carried at his soul level.

During another lifetime, this time in Sweden as my father, Manny left on his fishing boat early one morning, and never returned. I was his little girl waiting at the wharf, bereft and waiting and waiting for him to return. During our relationship in this lifetime, for his soul to restore balance it was essential to return to me after each parting. How I wished to share these insights with him.

It dawned on me that by travelling this part of my healing journey with Manny, I was able to leave when things became too intense. When I needed time to absorb the teachings, and to resolve them by accepting my part, I left the boat. I suspect that had I been living on land during all this processing, I would have taken the easy option of leaving and finding a new partner, perhaps learning nothing. I marvelled at our mutual depth of love and for sailing. The 'carrots' that kept bringing us back together on Kaleidoscope, each time beginning from a fresh perspective that increasingly came from our true nature.

Looking through this new lens of soul lessons at seemingly random events, in hindsight I recognised the serendipitous hand of my spirit guides.

Going back to the earliest weeks since Tim's accident, Geraldine's determination to connect me with Ishtar led me to Raman, who had opened the door to a life-changing new perspective. And the catamaran trip during our Queensland holiday that had rekindled my love of the ocean and prompted the unexpected impulse to learn to sail. This was followed by an irrational desire for global cruising, all crucial to reunite me with Manny. More recently, thanks to connecting with Marti, author Echart Tolle had explained the dark night of the soul, restoring my sanity. One thing was for sure - nothing was by chance.

Even my invented Corky persona served a role in these staged acts of divine interventions. Spurring me to adventures such as the crazy notion of joining a stranger on a yacht in a remote part of the planet. Although she had almost blocked the healing of my heart, she provided a potent illustration of my need to release acquired false beliefs about who I was.

Another intriguing point, my mentor said that imagination was the act of reaching into a realm of potential, and that if we imagined something, it already existed. Had I invented cavalier Corky, or was she an aspect of my soul, a former incarnation? I made a mental note to ask Raman if Manny and I had been pirates!

Excited about this new life I was creating, I felt ready for the next stage; to attend, mend and open my tattered, battered, heart.

Chapter 14

A NEW TAPESTRY

'We cannot pick up the same threads,
once we have put them down.
For a new tapestry is in the making.'

Screening the sun's glare with my hand shading my eyes, I follow the hawk's flight. Each effortless spiral in the updrafts reveals brown and cream feathery triangulations beneath its wings. Far above Lyttelton township, I look down on bustling miniature wharves extending like robot fingers into an enormous basin of green seawater. Colonial cottage roofs migrate out of the narrow streets into the low hillside slopes, seeking quietude. From my lofty height atop the steep volcanic crater, I watch my circling harbinger of change. The hawk appears each time a burgeoning piece of knowing soars into my awareness. It hovers nearby, rocking gently in the changing air currents as though cradling my fledgling consciousness.

FLYING IN THE FACE OF GRIEF   BY ANNWYN

Inwardly, I am learning to fly. Living once again in the familiar community of Lyttelton, I choose solitary walks in the hills rather than socialising in bustling cafes and pubs. Peaceful in my own company, I allow stillness into my life and, once again, I notice the messages from Spirit.

Awakening souls are often captivated by the notion of healing others, and I am no different. Unlike my mother, who places general practitioners on a pedestal, I choose alternative practices such as naturopathy and homeopathy as my pathway to wellness. Along the way, energy-based healing piques my curiosity and I make tentative inquiries about Reiki, colour therapy, acupuncture, and herbalism. Reiki has gained popularity, yet I don't feel a strong pull towards this modality. I stop looking, content for the time being that a seed has been planted.

Meanwhile, I begin the year teaching private students with learning difficulties at the Seabrook McKenzie Centre. I love working alongside these right-brained children who struggle in the left-brain school system, where creativity, intuition, and other modes of intelligence are often passed over in favour of regurgitated learning.

In the second school term, I exchange individual students for classroom teaching at the centre's small, specialised school, but within six weeks of accepting this position, I become unwell, to the point of being too exhausted to continue working. To focus on recovering my health, I resign from my teaching position, and with great reluctance, I visit my doctor.

"Ruth, what do the tests show?" I ask. I admire her shaved head and her black, pleated, full-length leather skirt. I also admire her ability to work alongside her patients' preferences.

"It's that thyroid of yours again. It's been underactive for these past nine years, but your herbal remedies have held it at bay. Except now, it has gone right off the chart, in the opposite direction."

"No wonder I sleep day and night."

Her face folds into empathy. "I know how much you dislike medical intervention. As it happens, in this case the best action is to monitor with regular readings until it rebalances itself. But you will need to rest. This could take weeks, even months, before we see any change," she cautions.

My doctor's prediction of a potential lengthy recovery is unacceptable to me — and also to a new, rather strange friend. "This will help," Brigid says in her throaty voice. "You will need to play it repeatedly. Not just once."

I turn the disc over in my hand, seeking a recognisable sign of legitimacy, and read the title aloud in a halting manner, "Tuning the Physical Instrument, by Energy Healer Judy Satori."

"You will find the vocalisation strange at first. Judy channels something called 'the sound of light.' It's pure energy healing, and you'll need to be open to it." Fixing me with her piercing blue eyes, she predicts the vibrational frequencies will rebalance my thyroid within a few weeks.

It takes effort to refrain from eye-sweeping the ceiling, hearing Laura's voice in my head saying, "Really, Mumsy?"

A few days later, curiosity gets the better of me. I open my window for fresh sea air, plump up my pillows, and get comfortable on top of the floral bedspread. Remembering Brigid's instructions, I close my eyes and take some deep breaths. I let out a long, peaceful sigh and settle down to listen.

Within seconds, my eyes fly wide open with shock as garbled, guttural utterings assault my ears and offend my intellect. I scramble off the bed and close the windows in case my neighbours hear. Furious with Brigid for suggesting this nonsense, it confirms my suspicion she is weird.

The next day, a nagging compulsion prompts me to give the CD another chance. My guides want me to get over myself and try again. Plus, I recall Raman saying that Tim also studied ancient forms of energy healing. I drop my judgmental resistance and open my mind and heart. This time, allowing the strange sounds to wash over me, I respond with the required openness. Becoming used to the strange sounds, I play the disc twice each day for two weeks until the next test results come in.

Doctor Ruth looks at the results on her computer, then back at me over the top of her glasses. "Annette, this is extraordinary. In just a few weeks, your thyroid has rebalanced. In fact, it's now in the optimal range."

I decide not to disclose my methods and return the CD to Brigid, along with a bottle of expensive champagne.

Knowing not to ignore this signpost, I peer down different streets for a modality to learn. It's a pity Reiki doesn't feel right for me, as several teachers in Christchurch offer this. Still getting the hang of my new way of living, I opt for security and return to private students on an individual basis, albeit not for long.

The universal machination of change never stops. Through their connections in the antiques business, Lea and Pav suggest an intriguing prospect. They propose I join a production team in the process of compiling 'The Alan Carter New Zealand Price Guide to Antiques & Collectables 2010'. My role would be three-fold: to contact and liaise with fifty antique dealers throughout New Zealand; drive a Sydney photographer around for five weeks; and write the description for each chair, vase, and plate photographed. They point out my former studies in the history of furnishings would help here. Without the faintest notion of why this random opportunity holds enormous appeal, I accept.

Willie, a small, wiry man, had been taking photographs of antiques for decades throughout Australia. Now, Carters extend their reach to New Zealand for the first time. We visit antique shops sprinkled around the South Island during school holidays and, after that, I abandon my students for two weeks to complete the job in the North Island. Soaking up the glorious autumnal scenery and meeting an array of eccentric antique shop owners rekindles my love of freedom. I feel reluctant to return to teaching. In truth, my heart no longer wants this. I now see the higher purpose of becoming unwell, followed by an out-of-the-blue chance to pull me away from teaching. Blown by the winds of change onto a different pathway, I cannot paste those autumnal leaves back on the tree. That tree no longer grows there.

Spirit loves to spread humour on soul-lesson sandwiches, and the irony of the road trip is not lost on me; it is the catalyst that maps out a new journey through life. All I need to do is notice and follow their strategically placed signposts. I discontinue tutoring my long-suffering students for the last time, not knowing how I will manage my financial requirements. Taking my second leap of faith, this time a healthy excitement for the unknown replaces my fears and vulnerability. I am learning to trust a new process of living life - surely the real meaning of an adventuress.

Within days of closing the door on my old life, 'by chance' I hear of a lesser-known energy healing modality called 'Magnified Healing.' Excitement ripples through me the moment I hear this name mentioned. Searching online, I learn that in the 1980s, two Californian women received this ancient practice as channelled information from Ascended Lady-Master Quan Yin. This eastern goddess lived a long life in China, revered for her qualities of longevity, love, compassion and forgiveness. Her spiritual status is likened to Mother Mary, and she is associated with healing the heart. No wonder my body responded with excitement!

Others in my circle have heard of Quan Yin, but not of Magnified Healing, and it takes six months to locate a German teacher who has taught this modality in Europe for ten years. She replies to my inquiry, saying I am the first person in New Zealand to ask about her weekend workshop of instruction and attunements. Lo and behold, within a fortnight, two other women inquire, and I book a flight to Wellington. I already hold an ardent desire to 'meet' Quan Yin despite having minimal idea of what this might involve.

The two other students are younger than me and also new to this. We admire each other's white flowing clothes that we were instructed to wear and inhale fragrant incense burning in the white-themed room. The experience already feels sacred and beautiful as Sabrina, our teacher, settles us in her crystal-filled healing clinic.

"Well, I am delighted to finally teach Magnified Healing in New Zealand." She beams at us. "After waiting ten years, three students appear out of thin air at the same time. But then, as we know, everything has its divine time. It appears Quan Yin wishes for her beautiful heart energies to be anchored here. Unlike many spiritual practices, which focus on the third eye, this ancient practice is experienced through the heart. Be assured if you invite the presence of Quan Yin into your energy field and make this a regular ritual, you will transform your life. Also, in this modality, Quan Yin collaborates with Mother Mary and Goddess Isis, making this a powerful, magnified triad of energies."

At first, I feel like a fish out of water gulping in airy quantum concepts. But over the next two days, Sabrina's words begin to make sense. She explains the components and functions of our human electrical circuitry, our chakras and auric field. I learn that we have several subtle fields of energy that extend beyond our physical body to make up our aura. When she explains how this energy system responds to our thoughts and emotions, I recall Raman's words about low or high vibrational frequencies, and finally connected some dots.

It becomes clear that if we take diligent care of our non-physical body, our physical body reflects this as good health. Sabrina demonstrates how to focus our attention on each chakra, directing beneficial energy to each associated area in our body. By the end of the first day, I experience my physical, mental, and spiritual body in a peaceful, balanced way as never before.

"Sabrina," I ask, "I understand how our chakras affect our physical body, but how do we heal, for example, grief in our heart?"

"Ah, as it happens, we are reaching this important part of our practice. Simply setting the intention to direct healing energy to your heart chakra is beneficial. That alone is a good thing to do. But we can amplify this by calling upon the powerful healing energies of Quan Yin. Remember, the heart is her specialised area. Within her vast consciousness, she embodies the heart qualities of cosmic love, forgiveness and compassion, also grace and mercy. When we align our intentions with her great reservoir of cosmic love, we magnify the outcome."

"Cosmic love?" all three acolytes chime in unison.

Sabrina smiles, "This means love without an agenda. Not the conditional love that most of humanity experiences, but the pure love from Source. Or God, whatever name you call the Creation Energy."

"But Quan Yin is no longer alive, right? I confess I am a bit confused by all of this," I say.

"Correct. But her energies and her consciousness are very much alive on Earth. Energy never dies. Also remember we are working with her collective energy. Which means that hundreds and thousands of souls also work with Quan Yin. It is like the Buddha collective, or the Christed collective. I repeat, energy never dies. We can invoke energy whenever we need it. This technique is so effective that the ascended masters have used it over eons. When you think about it, we are in fact working with quantum physics, because we invoke energies in a multi-dimensional manner that go beyond time and space. Does that help?"

With so much to absorb and making sure I understand, I ask, "So, I'm inviting the collective energies of Quan Yin into my heart?"

"Yes, that's it. And the heart energy of cosmic, or divine love, is the key to transforming our lives. Because heart energy is creation energy. Therefore, to create an optimal life, our hearts are invited to heal from grief, envy and betrayal - all the emotional wounds carried by humanity."

Her words strike a deep chord. Without thinking, my hands move into prayer position in the centre of my chest as a soundless sob escapes my lips. My eyes mist over with tenderness and gratitude for Tim, the depth of his gift dawning on me. I see how this noble journey of grief turns the spotlight on mental and emotional scars that would otherwise have remained hidden in the shadows for the remainder of my life. A tingling in my heart and at the top of my head concurs with that new insight. Opening my eyes, I see Sabrina and her other two students smiling at me with unbridled compassion. They, too, feel the palpable unconditional love of Quan Yin fill the small room and, at the same time, I think of a lotus whose petals have stayed shut for many years and now unfurl.

My initiation into the collective energy of Quan Yin proves to be pivotal in my life. I do not engage with this ascended master 'second-hand' through a channel. By holding a focused intention and inviting the energy of Quan Yin into my own energy field, I receive energy attunements direct from her. I channel her myself.

It is hard to believe the love, peace and happiness I feel. Never have I known such inner security. By resurrecting and reawakening my inner Babushka doll, I can see her layers now represent mind-body-spirit. Each layer requires tender healing to function and collaborate in its fullest measure. Through the incredible work Manny and I did together, I survived the rigours of healing my mental body. Now, held in Quan Yin's tender yet strong embrace, the wounds of my emotional body also heal. And when the mental and emotional bodies are healthy, the physical body spontaneously heals.

As every month passes, I move deeper into a state of calm, loving energy. After a full year of invoking Quan Yin every day and practising her healing modality, tangible results show. I look healthier and feel happier than I have been for decades. Others comment on my wellness, and one or two ask to learn the practice for themselves. My budding career as an energy healer and teacher begins, though not as far as my mother is concerned.

FLYING IN THE FACE OF GRIEF — BY ANNWYN

My mother's staunch Presbyterian views leave little space for us to meet, even as two adults. Our time together always begins with polite, superficial exchanges but soon deteriorates into a medieval clash between organised religion and spirituality. Mum considers me heading straight for hell.

At least, placated to learn my recent training sits under the blessing of Mother Mary, she agrees to a healing. Without meaning to deceive her, I phrase the modality in terms she will relate to. The three goddesses work as one unified field, but the mention of Quan Yin and Isis may confuse her - best to stick with Mother Mary and Jesus! Not understanding she is receiving a 'black-listed healing,' Mum quickly succumbs to the loving energies of Mother Mary.

"I love that music," she murmurs, referring to the high-vibrational instrumental sounds that support the healing. "It's almost angelic."

"Yes, it is. Close your eyes, Mum. Just relax. There's nothing for you to do but receive." Her face softens and sweetens, her breathing evens as I move through the invocations. Seldom do I see her at deep peace, her mind usually working in full battle mode, ready to fight over anything.

My heart reaches out to hers, but as I speak the next words, her eyes shoot open.

"Chakra! Did you say chakra?" she yells. "You tricked me!"

"Mum, chakras are just energy areas. Even Jesus, the greatest healer worked with chakras. They were called seals in the bible."

"You believe in Jesus?" she blinks, at a loss to match up so many disparities.

Her surprise at learning I welcome Jesus into my life is endearing. She has no idea our beliefs stem from the same source but have taken different routes.

Later that day I find a Presbyterian booklet next to my bed. Printed in black and white are the tell-tale signs of heresy, alerting my mother to vocabulary such as chakras, and to be wary of family members who gather in places other than churches. How I yearned for lush bush, abundant waterfalls, and the wild coastline of the Catlins, my tonic. It's time to take my leave. While saying our farewells the following day, mum asks if she might keep the Magnified Healing music CD.

During this time of consciously changing the way I do things, one of my new strategies has become a ritual of indulgence. I have developed a delightful habit of self-nurture after visits to my mother, an overnight stopover in a ruggedly beautiful area called the Catlins. Rather than seethe with irritation during the 600kms drive back to Christchurch, it's more productive to walk the windswept coastline until the dogmas of Mum's religious mindset have blown out to sea.

Wondering which of my two favourite hostels to stay at, I notice a low-flying hawk slightly ahead of me. It hovers directly in front of my car for a short distance before turning down a side road. Recognising a messenger, I follow in hot pursuit! Having pointed me in the right direction the hawk soon disappears and ten minutes later I discover a terrific hostel set on a farm in the middle of nowhere.

A delightful couple from Sweden, Karin and Omar, are the only other occupants. and soon we sit chatting in the late afternoon sun. Producing a bottle of wine, they accept a glass with enthusiasm and Omar fetches a bag of potato chips.

"How did you find this hidden place?" Karin is curious to know. "We didn't see it advertised."

"Neither did I. It sounds strange, but I followed a hawk," I laugh.

"What?" Omar almost spills his glass of wine. "I haven't heard anyone speak like that since I lived in Somalia."

"Oh yes, that hawk led me here was a messenger. Otherwise I would have kept on the main road and stayed at my usual place."

He leans forward with excitement, "My family consider hawks to be messengers too. Some of them were politically active. It was dangerous times in Somalia, and they had to travel on deserted roads to secret meetings. If there was an ambush waiting for them, a hawk would circle close by to warn them."

He falls silent after talking about the country he has fled. Grief floods his face and he pushes his wine glass away.

Karin squeezes his hand, white and black fingers entwine like piano keys. She tells me she had worked at a Swedish rehabilitation centre for refugees and had fallen in love with Omar. Trained as an English teacher, Karin is also a writer, in her words, of 'Mills & Boons' romantic fiction.

An avid reader, and wishing to change the subject she says, "I see so many Kiwis with their head in a book. On buses, at the beach, in cafes. We don't see that in Sweden. What are you reading at the moment, Annette?"

But I look at Omar instead. "I have known grief too. I can't imagine what you must have been through in Somalia." Water pools in the rims of his dark eyes, but I carry on. "And then having to leave your country of birth."

Karin nods. "Omar has been depressed at times. The things he saw."

"To answer your question, I'm devouring spiritual books. No romantic fiction for me," I joke. In a more serious tone, I add, "There is one that might help you, Omar."

A NEW TAPESTRY

Omar hangs onto every word when I talk at length about Echart Tolle, then says. "This conflict between our human ego and our higher nature. It sounds like the Sufi principles. Sufi is the mystical side of the Islamic religion I grew up with. I want to read this book," he said, picking up his wineglass again.

Laura observes the change within me and, although she has not yet dived so deep into her own grief, she's intrigued by my renewed vigour and happiness.

"Mumsy, are you telling me you can think about Tim, or hear his favourite Metallica song on the radio, and not have a meltdown?"

"Pretty much. Though I have to admit that 'Tears in Heaven' still gets me. When I can listen to that without blubbering, I will know I am free of grief."

"I can't imagine reaching that point,' she says, turning her head away."

"You were so young darling. And as well as human grief, you have soul grief to deal with. Remember, this is your first lifetime without him. In that respect, it has been much harder for you."

"I wish he could meet his niece and nephew. I wish they could know their uncle. I don't understand how you can feel at peace, Mum."

Pulling her close to my heart and moving damp strands of hair off her cheeks, I whisper, "Because my darling, I understand that on the soul level, we are never really apart. And I know now that I can choose to remember our beautiful boy with sorrow, or with love."

FLYING IN THE FACE OF GRIEF **BY ANNWYN**

Cupping her streaked face in my hands, "I choose love." She nods and sniffs against my shoulder. I know she is a long way from that, but I also know I'm in a much stronger position to help her get there.

Chapter 15

SOUL KEYS

'Like a pottery shard uncovered
in an archaeological dig,
each fragment inspires further
excavation — more of my inner sacred site.'

According to my recent dabbling in numerology, the year 2009 represents number eleven. And, being a master number, eleven carries an amplified significance. Described as a cosmic door that unlocks spiritual awareness and inner wisdom, it makes perfect sense to associate this number with spiritual teachers, leaders, and philosophers. Hardly surprising then, even inevitable, that another ascended master arrives to feed my insatiable appetite for spiritual knowledge.

Almora's gentle energy feels familiar; it reminds me of Raman. During channelled gatherings held each month, he immerses his audience in long-forgotten wisdom. His over-arching message about humanity's true divine nature dovetails with my burgeoning awareness of my authentic self. Now, with my wild, wounded human nature tamed, space opens for my soul to speak and to be heard. I want to know more. I want to become more. Making a conscious decision to dedicate my life to my spiritual development, I book regular private sessions with this illuminating teacher.

To my surprise, I carry many more wounds requiring healing, all from previous incarnations. Almora navigates the way through several significant lifetimes, smoothing rough edges off embedded scars. In each case, it is necessary to reach back into the scenario of those former times and access the feelings of conflict and distress. Under this two-pronged healing and tutelage of Almora and Quan Yin, associated emotions of fear stored in my cellular memory transmute into love, allowing more of my innate, higher nature to emerge.

Like a pottery shard uncovered in an archaeological dig, each fragment inspires me to excavate more of my inner sacred site. No longer limited by my acquired human identity, getting to know myself as an ancient vessel of wisdom thrills me. It feels like being introduced to a neighbour I've lived next door to all my life but have never spoken with. Now we are on each other's doorsteps, wondering why we've taken so long to meet.

Many of my soul lessons in this lifetime focus on rebalancing disempowerment experienced within marriage, as clergy, and even as a slave during previous incarnations. This wasn't necessarily a personal characteristic of partners or colleagues; rather, it was a consequence of social norms of the day that often held an unequal distribution of power and resources. Such as the lifetime with Manny when we both suffered disempowerment through poverty. Yet, we were all involved, playing agreed roles with diligence to evolve through and beyond our human condition. And we all made our choices regarding the situations and circumstances we found ourselves in. Environments, genders, and roles changed like movie scenes, yet the overriding areas of learning remained the same.

Thus, a plethora of opportunities have been created in my current lifetime to transmute unbalanced power within relationships. Gallant Manny providing my greatest challenges and gifts for my greatest area of learning. Armed with this insight, I understand that our human dramas are opportunities for soul growth. Except we do not know that until we awaken to the presence of our soul. And there's the rub.

Nothing is for nothing. The events that 'happen to us' convey an invitation to transcend the drama. I realise now that life doesn't 'happen' to us; it happens 'because' of us. It could be a mental, emotional, physical, or spiritual challenge — like each layer of my Babushka doll undergoing a rigorous overhaul. Observing others, I note that, like me, they are adepts in some areas and novices in others. We are all working through our carefully orchestrated soul lessons to restore balance. And we learn from each other. When I needed to learn self-empowerment, Manny turned up to teach me because of his mastery in that particular domain.

Nine years have passed. My amateur understanding of numerology reveals number nine as 'completion energy'. I decide to ask Tim what this means for me and, as usual, get more than I ask for.

"Well done, Mumsy. You have almost completed your soul awakening stage. You now understand the difference between your human nature and your higher nature."

"Almost?"

"Yes. Now you will be 'tested' to use human words. Think of it as an initiation into the next stage." He pauses and laughs saying, "I can see your eyes rolling, you know."

"You mean there is more?"

He gives a belly laugh. "Oh yes, there is always more. Even for God."

"What will I have to do?"

"The initiation will occur in a natural way. Don't worry, I've got your back. By the way, are you still in contact with Manny?"

"Sometimes we exchange news. Why?"

"You might want to alert him about a Tsunami warning for Fiji."

Even though I expect him to already know about the warning, I email Manny straight away. But he hasn't heard and, grateful for the extra time, he sails to a safe anchorage to prepare. A few days later, he emails to confirm his safety and surprises me with an invitation to sail Kaleidoscope back to New Zealand. My fingers can't type fast enough!

But within days of Manny's invitation, apprehension swallows my excitement. I haven't seen Manny for eighteen months; another nine. Irrational thoughts and scenarios disturb me. I pace the room, scolding myself for being ridiculous, and land heavily in an armchair which thuds against the wall. The impact dislodges a framed photograph of Tim hanging above my head, which lands literally in my lap.

Holding his image in my hands, I tell him my worries about the upcoming reunion with Manny. Tim is twelve years old in the photograph, but that doesn't stop me from pouring out my heart in earnest.

"What was I thinking, Tim? It's been a year and a half since we were last together. I've changed so much. Radically changed. I'm not sure I can be honest about my new spiritual beliefs. You know what he's like. What if he thinks it's another invented persona? Will he think I've swapped my human ego for spiritual ego? Like one of those phony spiritual healers that get found out. I'm a healer!"

I pause to imagine the scene, sipping a sundowner — Einstein and Nietzsche on his side of the cockpit, Tim and Almora on mine. "What evidence do I have for my beliefs?" I wail. "And, to top it off, I'm terrified about the sea passage. How crazy is that? It's never worried me before."

Exhausted from my emotional woes, I drift into a fitful doze until the ringing telephone lands me back in the chair. Deidre, a girlfriend and neighbour, invites me for a pot of herbal tea at the Volcano Café. Still dazed, I begin to decline but hear myself agreeing to join her.

Ra, Tim's best friend, sets down the cups and teapot on our table, then gives me a big hug. Now twenty-seven years old, he works part-time at the café to support his fledgling business in high fashion for men. He looks every bit the artistic designer, his pointed goatee beard emphasising fine cheekbones. His elegant hands suggest an air of refinement, but I sense his irreverent playfulness remains. He and Tim used to fill our house with uncontrollable laughter, finding humour in the mundane. I relax, already glad Spirit made me come.

Before I can discuss what troubles me, Deidre leans in and says, "Tim is very present. He's got some things to tell you." Tim often imparted messages through Deidre, who comes from a family skilled with insightful intuition; it is not by chance she suggested tea at 8pm on a Wednesday night.

"First of all, don't worry about the ocean passage. It will be great, but you must not leave Fiji until a storm has passed. It won't be detected by weather stations."

"Oh! Perhaps that's why I was worried about the passage. My higher self knows about the storm."

"Exactly," Deidre confirms, then continues. "Now, Tim says to be absolutely honest with Manny. You must be direct in your speech, no tiptoeing around on eggshells. He'll be there whenever you need backup, and he says to always keep these sage words in mind, 'Who cares and so what!'"

I burst into laughter at his unexpected advice. He shares other pieces of information, including the importance of Ra's friendship to him. He asks me not to tell Ra this, as he is not yet able to receive such a message.

With Tim sitting in the seat next to me, the plane lands at Suva Airport. Manny appears in good health and spirits, content to be a single hander again. Within hours of arriving on board, I recognise the first potential trigger. I state my views from my new spiritual awareness, hold my breath, and wait for a lightning bolt to strike me down. Manny responds with cynicism at first, but with Tim's comical yet empowering strategy, I resist engaging with the trivial.

'Who cares and so what!' becomes my default while Manny and I wrestle our wills for a few days, adjusting to new dynamics. But having dropped so many layers of my fragile, defensive ego, nothing remains to challenge.

Manny accepts Tim's weather message, even after I divulge my source of the storm warning. The yachts leaving for New Zealand, believing they have a perfect weather window, encourage others to depart too. Two days later, Manny calls out for me to come and listen to the conversations on the German radio network. The yachties are dealing with severe winds and high waves, and one yacht breaks its mast. His eyes twinkle as he says in his soft, husky way, "Thanks, Tim."

Alone on deck one night, watching the moonlight dance on Kaleidoscope's foamy wake, I contemplate the magnitude of grief. There are so many aspects to unravel. On all levels, it involves a rite of passage across oceans of erroneous beliefs.

Lulled by the boat's rhythm, quietude envelops me, and a familiar presence appears. I recognise Centatron, the guide who came to me after my dark night of the soul with his Babushka doll analogy. His role seems to be one of affirming and summing up for me after significant growth.

"Greetings, Beloved. You and Manny have indeed crossed oceans together on many levels. The most important part of your healing occurs each time you both take responsibility for your own pain, your own human frailties, and your own wounds."

Centatron stays silent for a while. Small waves tap at the hull, and I feel Tim tapping at my heart as Centatron conveys the last part of his message.

"I want to emphasise, Beloved, that your mental body sabotaged the grieving process, especially when you relaunched yourself as the swashbuckling Corky. We, in the spirit realms, knew this defense strategy would delay your recovery. Because the transmutations of old wounds can only occur when accepting that pain comes from self; the healing could not come from your persona of Corky. But realise, Beloved, that you had agreed to create this experience in order to show others.

"You have searched your soul, done the work, and found the love."

Within that soul search, I found the love of my true nature and in doing so, I found my son. I cracked the code, the deceptively simple code that unlocks the door to the nonphysical realms of a soul's eternal love. Soul love is different from sentimental human love created through conditions and expectations that can be withdrawn at a moment's notice. At the soul level, there is no drama. There is no traumatic separation. There, I hold Tim sweetly in my heart with constancy and commune with ease through telepathic thoughts and vibrational frequencies. There I feel his love, breathe in his excitement, and drink his inspiration.

Literally wearing this newfound love on my sleeves, fifty shades of pink fill my wardrobe in 2010. Even though pink isn't fashionable, I can't stop my feminine side from twirling out of the closet. For years, out of necessity I have drawn on my masculine qualities as provider and protector of my children. Now I revel in the softer qualities of the divine feminine that my healed heart naturally embraces and gravitates to.

For me, Quan Yin epitomises the divine sacred feminine and, in part, I credit my energy shift to her graceful and loving manner. Her heart exudes strong, compassionate, nurturing energies capable of spontaneously healing and expanding the hearts of others.

While my healing practice grows, I sell collectibles at the Saturday Lyttelton market to supplement my income. Every item on the stall provides an outlet for my reclaimed femininity and is inspired by the maxim of English designer William Morris, that 'all things in the home must be both beautiful and practical'. The artisan designer witnessed the burgeoning machine age of the 1800s, which mass-produced ugly items with straight lines. Affronted by the denial of graceful, feminine curves observed in nature, he revitalised handcrafted furniture and soft furnishings. Morris's exquisite, nature-filled designs remain popular today.

Meanwhile, there is great excitement among Almora's students at the announcement of two events. The first is a gathering at a remote, rugged location in the middle of the South Island called Castle Hill, and said to be the heart chakra of New Zealand. The second is a serendipitous pilgrimage to Glastonbury, England, the heart chakra of the entire planet.

"What's so special about Glastonbury?" Laura asks.

"I don't have the foggiest notion. All I know is that wild horses couldn't keep me away."

"You're going across the globe without knowing why? Mumsy!"

Feeling sheepish, I reply, "Actually, there is an exceptionally good reason to go. I can do the advanced level of Magnified Healing. There's one in Ireland, just a few days after the pilgrimage ends."

"I can see you are determined. Have you talked about it to Mr. Who Cares and So What? I've been using that too," she grins.

"First things first. Let's see how it goes at Castle Hill."

"It's going to be cold up there, Mumsy. A stone's throw from the southern alps. You're mad!"

"Ah well, it's the winter solstice, a powerful date to be in a place like that. I'm excited!"

Laura is right. I'm mad. Huffing into my knitted gloves to warm my hands before shoving them back in my pockets, it's the crack of dawn and I wonder why I'm not snug in my bed. At least I have warm ears, unlike the eerie stone giants towering over me, wearing their hats of snow.

"I would kill for a coffee," I mutter to those in earshot.

Our facilitator hears our muffled giggles. "No talking please," she scolds, making us want to laugh louder, but we assume a reverent manner.

Snow crunches and sighs under our boots as we slowly wend our way through the labyrinth of soaring stones, guided by the thin ray of torchlight. Relieved our gathering point is sheltered, I shuffle into my place among twelve others, our faces blotchy with cold. We encircle an oblong-shaped slab of limestone that rests on the ground, and two of the women light tall candles inside glass lanterns, placing them alongside several crystals. Another arranges a garland of flowers and ferns, and another lights cones of incense. This is my first ceremony at a sacred site and I take it all in, not knowing what to expect.

Our facilitator begins by invoking the *kaitiaki*, the guardians and keepers of wisdom at this sacred site, known also at Kura Tawhiti, a faraway place of learning. Her high, reedy voice is thinned by the cold and barely audible, yet there is no doubting her sincerity.

"We greet the ancient gods of this sacred place. We honour the Stone People with gratitude for the opportunity to commune and connect with their wisdom."

Standing ankle-deep in snow, my feet painfully cold, it's hard to focus on ancient gods. But, remembering I'm in a stone library holding rare knowledge, I push thoughts of chilblains aside and concentrate.

One of the women chants an incantation to help us forget our discomfort so we may enter the portals of our hearts. The place where dimensions and realities collide. At first, I'm distracted, but I gradually leave my physical state and enter a higher level of consciousness. The energies are palpable; I feel them as pressure on my chest and slowness of breath. I peer through my eyelashes for a moment to watch curling tendrils of mist spiralling in front of my face. I breathe deeper. Slower. Silence roars in my ears like a rush of wind.

Then all is peaceful—but not for long.

I'm vaguely aware that my feet are warming up. *How curious, and what a blessing*, I think. The warmth builds, intensifying into heat. It's as though someone is stoking a furnace beneath the Earth. The soles of my feet are on fire now, and I lift one foot and then the other as though the snow will put out the blaze. I'm aware of the chafing noise that my parka is making as I hop about like silver on a smithy's forge. Bewildered, I take my boots off and stand in the snow in stocking feet, but this makes no difference at all. How I long for frozen toes and chilblains now!

After what seems an agonisingly long time, others stretch their bodies as they return from their journeys. A talking stick is passed around the circle and each of us speaks of our experience. Some describe fantastic visions of cosmic beings shimmering in gold, while others proclaim profound insights. All I felt was my feet burning like toast.

Dreading my turn, I take the stick in both hands and begin by apologising. "I'm sorry for my distracting behaviour. It sounds weird, but my feet were scorching. I felt as though my feet were Sunday's roast."

Chortles ripple around the group. When it is calm again, to my surprise, I discover I have clarity around what occurred. Without hesitating, I tell them, "It was Gaia sending up energies from her core. She activated the chakras in the soles of my feet for future work. She says that in the years to come,

FLYING IN THE FACE OF GRIEF   **BY ANNWYN**

I will travel to her sacred sites around the planet to activate portals that have cycles of activity and dormancy."

Brushing away tears, I share the second part of her message. "She's asking me to understand that I'm not a visual seer, but that I have other gifts. She says I see with my feelings and my body."

I feel Tim's presence behind me and hear him say, *Nice work, Mumsy. Another beginning.*

Making my way back to the lodge for hot drinks and breakfast, I'm brimming with excitement. A young woman falls in beside me and pushes her hood back, her dark eyes bright as she says, "I'm so glad you shared your story. I have often felt disappointed when not seeing. Today, I realised I have the same gifts as you."

A few weeks later, an email arrived with a photograph attached. One member of our group, a professional photographer, had been shaken out of his meditation and was prompted to take a shot while the rest of us were still journeying. In this photograph, not one person is recognisable. All that can be seen in the numinous light of Kura Tawhiti, suspended between night and day, is a sphere of golden lights and tall white flames.

As the pilgrimage date draws closer and, acting on Laura's prompt, I close my eyes, still my mind, and bring Tim into my awareness. I often sense him waiting in an armchair for me, long legs dangling over the arm. At times I experience him as my son, and at other times I experience him as the evolved soul that he is. On this occasion, I feel an unusual reluctance from him to discuss Glastonbury with me.

I tease, "Well, someone's keeping a lid on things."

"You will understand, my dear mother, that some things are best left unknown. It's all in the timing. I do know that Glastonbury will have quite an impact. It's one of Earth's most sacred places, the heart chakra of Gaia, if you like. You would not feel the call to visit this place of transformation if you had not healed your heart. It's not by chance that Quan Yin calls you to do this inner healing. It has opened many doors."

"Have you and I shared a previous life there?" I want to know, feeling a slight unease.

"I'm not permitted to share that yet." He softens his voice, "But there is one thing I can share with you. It's big Mumsy."

Chapter 16

GAIA'S HEART

*'I sob for the frail abbot,
dragged up the slopes of the Tor
to gallows on that hallowed, sacred land.'*

It isn't by chance that my friend Victoria and I arrive a day earlier than the rest of our group. Walking back to our lodgings in Glastonbury that first afternoon, I spy a tiny 14th-century chapel down a narrow alley. Worn flagstones lead to an enchanting walled garden with borders of roses and lavender, separated by a strip of green lawn. The front wall of the chapel glows with sunlight striking the small diamond panes of glass in the deep recessed windows. How different from its grimy street-side wall, blackened by years of traffic fumes, which disguises its sacred purpose.

"Vic, let's go in. It's dedicated to Mary Magdalene. Funny how I've become intrigued by her all of a sudden. My mother used to call her a prostitute."

"She repeated the church's story. You go ahead, but I'm going to get some sun. It feels like this one is for you. Take your time." She yawns and stretches out on a beckoning wooden bench.

Vic is right; I do feel drawn. Vic's intuition sharpens when she is with me. Somehow, our combined energies amplify her sight.

The iron bolt rattles across the lock, and the heavy oak door creaks open. An uncommon stillness tingles up my spine in the candle-lit stone chapel. Taking tentative steps across the flagstones toward the altar, the candles splutter and a presence engulfs me. A compassion-blanket of love bundles me up like a glorious shawl of joy and gratitude. Bewildered and humbled by this outpouring of love, I fall to my knees, sobbing tears of joy – and, for reasons unknown, relief!

I sense a homecoming, a greeting by those who have missed my absence for a very long time. Of course, I can't know this, but I feel it. Still on my knees, I bathe in those exquisite energies until I intuitively understand this as the presence of Mary Magdalene. I will meet her again in the Wells Cathedral, when she channels a message for our group through me.

In the meantime, our tour guide, John Flanagan, collects the other five group members from London and gathers us under his Irish wings. For the next seven days, he escorts us to iconic sacred sites in Somerset and Cornwall. We meditate in soaring cathedrals, crumbling monastic ruins, and damp earth barrows. We sing in stupendous stone circles and sit in silence in the strange crop circles. Each evening, we return to the small town of Glastonbury and share our day.

Almora prepares us to be sensitive to the energies of these ancient places. He explains how we might feel or sense events that have taken place hundreds, if not thousands of years ago. Glastonbury is the intersecting point of masses of energy ley lines and here, the veils are said to be thin. People often step into other realities; I marvel at the physical and the non-physical aspects of it all. But after my exquisite encounter with Mary Magdalene, I don't expect anything else to happen to me. I would be quite happy to press my nose against the shop windows in High Street, peering at crystals, cosmic clothing and witches' broomsticks.

In the tradition of modern-day pilgrims, we begin on the crest of Wearyall Hill, above Glastonbury Village. After a gratitude meditation for our safe journey from New Zealand, we add our ribbons to the profusion of clooties, the bright scraps of cloth, tied to the legendary Thorn tree.

John explains in his lilting Irish accent, "It's said that Joseph of Arimathea brought twelve Essenes who were closest to Jesus, with him to Avalon, as it was called then, for safety. Earlier on, Jesus gave his uncle a Thorn tree staff, which Joseph stuck in the earth before spending the first night on the hill. By morning, the staff had sprouted buds and taken root in the ground. Joseph saw this as a sign that his Essene community would flourish here. This tree is a descendant and honours the sacrifices of pilgrims."

Enchanted by the legend, I stand up to leave, but my legs collapse beneath me. Embarrassed, I struggle to stand. "Come on, old lady," laughs Victoria. She offers her hand and hauls me up, a huge grin on her face. But after teetering a few steps, I fold in a heap.

"I'll be all right. You go ahead with the others. I'll meet you outside the abbey." After a few minutes, my legs cooperate and I hurry down the hill to catch up with our babbling group under the arched entrance of the monastery.

FLYING IN THE FACE OF GRIEF BY ANNWYN

As we move through the abbey's antechamber, a wide, high-walled lane pulls us out of busy Magdalene Street, and the chatter stops. We exchange expectant glances. The unmistakable shift from the town's hustle to the monastic hanging quietude hints at numinous energies that lie ahead.

Our group heads for the hub of this medieval monastery, the abbot's personal kitchen. We pass jutting, broken arches and lines of stone footings that hint at their former purpose. Yet the kitchen remains complete, a square and a circle form the building's unique shape. From the outside, it looks like a stone square with low walls, with an inverted hooped skirt of grey roof tiles placed on the top. At the apex sits an oversized slate bonnet that keeps rain out of open vents.

Seated on a hard wooden bench, my feet brushing the flagstone floor, I breathe in the claggy air. I count eight architectural ribs supporting the underskirts of the octagonal-shaped roof. Lime-washed walls draw my gaze to the highest point of the ceiling, where natural light comes through a 'bonnet' that protects the open ventilation lantern from rain.

A bossy female voice announces the arrival of a plump, red-faced cook, holding a wriggling boy by the scruff of his neck. Ignoring us, she barks at her assistant, "Each corner 'as its own kind of cookin' - roastin' there, bakin' there, and boilin' in this one 'ere. That one over there's for washin' up." She shoves the lad in the direction of her fleshy finger, "Wash yer filthy hands. Fetch the flour. The milk. Be quick."

Breadmaking soon gets underway with drifts of flour intent on escaping her rough hands. The lad, who receives boxed ears just for being hapless would like to escape too.

"See, this whole kitchin was built like a big chimney. Got no wood in that roof. She won't ever burn down." She pauses to check the lad's head for nits, sending me and the rest of the audience into hysterics. "We got everythin' we need right 'ere. Fish for our dear abbot. Saffron salmon for him. He don't eat much flesh even though he enjoys the hunt. There's venison from our deer parks, fit for King Henry. You won't go hungry here, laddie boy. Just as well, with them blimin' lords and pilgrims coming all the time expecting to be fed. Ooh, my poor feet," she complains, her ampleness now overhanging a sturdy oak stool.

"We feed beggars Tuesdays and Fridays. Nobility every day of the week. One time, five hundred at one sitting. And the horses housed an' all. Known for our lavish hospitality here at Glaston. Well, we would be, wouldn't we? Wealthiest abbey in the county, aren't we."

She pauses to slap the drowsy boy into alertness before boasting, "Even Jesus and his uncle Joseph came here. Of course, that happened long before the abbey existed. But they came here. Go and fetch some walnuts, laddie."

With her servant out of the kitchen, our cook's attention turns to her audience. She picks Victoria to help her, whose pretence of objecting to having her hair checked for nits earns her a place facing the corner with her hands behind her back. I become embarrassed by my response to the cook's antics and tales, each regale sending me into uncontrollable fits of laughter. It becomes touch and go between tears streaming down my face and leaking down my legs. I find her humour hysterical, but no one else seems to find her quite as hilarious as I do. Somehow, her nuances and jokes sound familiar and alive to me. I could sit there all day peeling potatoes while listening to her stories.

The laughter dies down, and our bustling bread maker stops at her bench. She places her floury hands palms down on the heavy oak table to steady herself, then begins to relay the dreadful events that occurred one mid-November morning in 1539.

In a hushed, trembling voice, she begins. "There was a great to-do in the north porch. King Henry's men wanted to see our dear old abbot. But he was resting at his grange, Sharpham Manor. We 'ad to call him back 'ere, bless 'im. They started tearing down the walls. They were looking for somethin'. They took our abbot to London. Put 'im in the tower. Shame on them."

Twisting the corners of her apron and sniffling, she says, "The king's commissioners claimed to have found treasures and documents secreted in the abbey's stone walls. Along with his treasurer and sacrist, they charged Abbot Whiting with treason and stealing from Glastonbury Church." She weeps noisily into her soiled sleeve. The sight of their abbot dragged on a wooden gate behind two horses, through the muddy streets of Glastonbury, had affected the townsfolk deeply. Their abbot provided spiritual leadership and assured their well-being.

Even though my rational mind knows this is 'just a play', my heart lurches with compassion. Hot tears slide down my cheeks as I picture Abbot Whiting dragged all the way up the slopes of the Tor, where gallows await him on that hallowed land. As the cook's words describe his brutal death, my body begins to jerk with violent spasms. Deep sobs rack my body, becoming as uncontrollable as my former mirth. My friend, Janine, places her hand on my knee, but I am inconsolable.

My story, preserved in these stones for nearly five hundred years, reveals itself with crystal clarity in less than five minutes. The secrets of the lime-washed walls speak loudly this day. I know without a doubt that I lived the life of Richard Whiting, the last abbot of Glastonbury Abbey.

Dazed, I listen to the gruesome details. First, they hung the poor man on the gallows, just enough to break his neck, but not to kill him. After castration, they opened his torso and removed his heart and entrails. They then took him down to decapitate and quarter his body. His four limbs were boiled in tar and displayed on the gates of the four nearest towns, as a deterrent to any further dissent. As a further warning to the Glastonbury folk, they placed their abbot's head on a spike above the ruins of his beautiful abbey.

Although I can still hear the cook's voice, it now comes from a distant place. Chilled to the bone, I shake with shock. Unable to listen to anymore, I stagger outside, dry retching and gasping for air. I sit on the ground sobbing with disbelief. A warm tingling in my heart alerts me to Tim's presence, reminding me of three words he gave me before leaving New Zealand. He simply said, 'It's big, Mumsy.'

Pulling myself together, I walk on shaking legs towards three friends, who now stand around the high altar of the great church. But as I near them, an invisible, impenetrable wall bars me from going further. Like a powerful shield holding dread and grief, it obstructs my path. My strength drains and I feel nauseous. I can't move past it. Exhausted by the intensity of my emotions, I huddle into a recessed stone wall and weep. Despite this swirling confusion, I know I must confront these ugly, crafted, dark energies.

Several times I try to walk through the ruined archway but am forced to turn back every time. The energies are strong. They feel real. Victoria hovers a short distance ahead of me, desperate to pull me through 'the wall' and comfort me. Buoyed by her huge heart willing me on, I double my willpower, call on Quan Yin, and stagger towards the High Altar.

FLYING IN THE FACE OF GRIEF   BY ANNWYN

At the rectangular-shaped piece of ground, where yellow dandelions flourish, the three women surround me in a tight circle. Understanding what has occurred, they have remained to invoke healing energies by chanting long, sonorous notes, the ancient art of toning, and channelling light language. Their multidimensional language of light catapults me into another state of consciousness where twelve priestesses encircle me.

The rest of our group is now on the other side of the abbey grounds, resting under a tree by a large, lily-filled pond. We join them in meditation to honour the many Celtic Goddesses. I sense these ancient spirits continuing the deep healing begun by the High Altar. Quan Yin joins them and her exquisite lavender healing colour fills my heart and mind's eye.

With a free hour allotted for lunch, most of the women take the opportunity to shop. Janine and I opt for a quiet lunch, but still shaken by the morning's events, I can't eat. Our next sacred site, the Chalice Well Gardens, soothes my discombobulated state. I wander through towering trees, smell late roses, and bathe my feet at the pool in King Arthur's Court.

Still in this shady part of the extensive gardens, our group sits around on steps and benches to meditate. A woman with the gift of sight whispers that Tim wishes to speak with me. Longing to chat, I tune in but can't hear or feel him. Desperate to feel his presence, I weep.

Later, Almora told me this scene held profound significance for Tim, that he yearned to be with me on the physical plane. An additional level to this emotional scene surprises me. It was an initiation marking Tim's final release of emotional attachment to his former life on Earth.

He would no longer feels sorrow from not being physically with loved ones.

That night, memories of the 16th-century events flood back into my awareness with intensity. Although spared the visual version, I can't escape the emotional waves of horror and fear. I feel the deepest grief, comparable to losing my darling son ten years earlier. Victoria does her best to calm me, but trauma waves roll in throughout the night. At my lowest ebb, I cry like a child, pleading to 'go home'. Not New Zealand, but to my home in the spirit realm. I've seen more than enough of the brutality of the Dark Ages.

When morning light overtakes the night's darkness, I can't face the thought of joining our group. Tim delivers a stern message through Vic that I need to stay in bed for a few hours while he continues healing me. As it happens, Victoria and I had already visited the morning's destination of Tintagel. Janine confirms the inkling I have that I must return to the abbey when she arrives with two pieces of pounamu. Holding out the sacred greenstone of New Zealand in her palm, she says, "You will know where to bury them."

Deep sleep claims me until midday. The luxury of a long shower followed by Quan Yin's healing technique makes a world of difference. Having toured Ireland and Cornwall with Victoria for several weeks, I appreciate having time by myself. Stashing a dining room teaspoon into my bag, I walk with tentative steps to the abbey, afraid I will encounter the ghastly memories again.

I begin in the safety of the abbey's museum. Fragments of cobalt-blue glass, which once drew light through majestic windows, fascinate me. A dark blue velvet cape, pinned onto a wall behind glass, hangs like a huge butterfly with wings embroidered with golden thread. I gaze at the fine needlework, wondering if I once wore this exquisite garment.

Feeling braver, I venture out into the abbey grounds where gentle rain has reduced the crowds. Walking with calm intent, I return to the 'trauma wall', relieved to find it feels peaceful.

This time, I savour the wonder of one of England's most celebrated abbeys as I move among the ruins, admiring the remaining elaborate masonry. Beyond King Arthur's tomb and then further again beyond the High Altar, I come to the area where the abbey's most recent addition, the Edgar Chapel, once stood. I notice a plaque in the form of a small white cross bearing the name, 'Richard Whiting'. Looking upon my former name with curious detachment, I understand this to be a previous incarnation, a former lifetime on Earth, which surfaces momentarily for healing, and that is that. Done and dusted.

Next to the cross sits a large rock known as 'Solomon's Stone', under which I place a piece of pounamu. With the assistance of the teaspoon, I bury the other piece amongst the dandelions on the site of the High Altar. I ask Mother Earth to receive these precious healing stones into her care.

Finding a quiet corner in a café to sip weak English coffee, I reflect on the previous day. Indicators had shown something was brewing: the encounter with Mary Magdalene and the curious sense of relief; and my legs buckling at the Thorn tree. But being inexperienced with such things, I didn't understand these portents. I envied the women in my group gifted with clairvoyant sight, who said my inner vision was gnostic, received through feelings and knowing.

While visiting Stonehenge, we mark Tim's twenty-seventh birthday. That's another nine - the penny drops regarding his completion by detaching emotionally from his loved ones. I lay a huge bunch of bright sunflowers on a large flat stone. After experiencing the various energies of the megalithic stones, the women form a large sharing circle. Standing with my feet planted on England's ancient land, I ask my friends to honour my son by singing him 'Happy Birthday'. Delighted at this light-hearted idea, they sing a rousing song that reverberates through the giant stones. A huge burst of playful energy fills my body, followed by the extraordinary sensation of being lifted high into the air. I suspect life will never be the same again!

Within days of stumbling into my previous lifetime at the abbey, someone hacks down the Thorn Tree on Wearyall Hill. This symbolic act had happened once before, decades ago, and our group are shocked along with the folk of Glastonbury. Could this current act of sabotage be connected to energies stirred up by my recalled memories?

Supported by Almora, it will take two years to retrieve and heal emotional and mental wounds inflicted during the lifetime of the Glastonbury abbot. His death so heinous, my soul had buried it deep beneath my human conscious awareness.

Chapter 17

CITY OF LIGHT

'Eleven years ago, a kind stranger watched Tim's soul leave his body. During the earthquakes I held space for strangers in the same way.'

*M*assive, relentless earthquakes continue to rock the city according to the Irish television reporter. Sipping tea in the foyer of my small Dublin hotel, I glance up at the screen, catching up with world news while browsing through tourist brochures. For twelve days, my attention has been occupied by the Glastonbury pilgrimage, followed by advanced training in Magnified Healing. Disinterested, I cock my head to catch a glimpse of the shaken city, but my casual observance turns to shock when a familiar building fills the screen; the iconic Christchurch Cathedral from my hometown in New Zealand. I sit riveted to the scene of huge masonry blocks scattered around the base, as though the cathedral has allowed its petticoat to fall around its feet before stepping out of it. The hotel receptionist says that after the

FLYING IN THE FACE OF GRIEF **BY ANNWYN**

first 7.1 quake on September 4th, she has watched nothing else for the past four days. A cold shiver slithers over each vertebra as my mind dashes to the disturbing experience at Glastonbury Abbey ruins just days earlier. My intuition tells me Laura is safe. All the same, it is a relief to speak to her later that day and learn Lyttelton has emerged from the quakes with minor damage.

On my return to Christchurch four weeks later, black stuff still oozes out of the streets, drying into thick black dust that fouls the air and sticks to trees and buildings. My snug rented Lyttelton cottage is unharmed, but ten weeks later, a mere ten seconds changes that.

Since returning from Glastonbury, I have volunteered each Tuesday in a city spiritual centre as an energy healer. Close to 1 pm on a scorching hot day of February 22nd, 2011, I sit meditating in a room filled with soothing fragrance and music. It is my customary preparation to attain a tranquil state before invoking Quan Yin and other spirits who assist with clients. Without warning, my chair bucks like a horse and I sprawl onto the floor. All hell breaks loose as an invisible wrecking ball slams the building with a deafening roar.

Drilled since childhood to crouch beneath a table or stand under a doorway during an earthquake, my gut instinct says, "Get out!" It is impossible to stay upright, so I crawl on hands and knees through glass popping out of buckled window frames, dodging large cabinets sliding around the floor. Scrambling outside unscathed, I find hundreds of people huddled in the middle of the road where water gushes out of fissures. The low-rise buildings in this area are several blocks from the central business district and, although buckling and swaying, they stay intact. An astonished cry goes up as a huge dust storm soars above the inner city, resembling the mushroom effect of a nuclear explosion. More dust clouds rise skyward as Christchurch falls to its knees.

For a while, people gabble like geese, speculating on the safest thing to do. Others stand silent, checking their phones and all the while casting nervous glances at the ominous umbrella in the sky. We can only guess at the impact of this foreboding sight.

A peculiar thing happens. I spy a friend I haven't seen for several years walking in my direction, holding a bunch of envelopes in one hand. I know she works in an inner-city high-rise building for a lawyers' firm. She appears to be looking about for a mailbox as though nothing has happened. Spotting me in the crowd, she waves and comes closer with shock and confusion showing on her face. Used to seeing her tanned and looking years younger than her sixth decade, I gasp at this ancient woman standing in front of me. Resembling a brown walnut with lines etched into her face, she has aged a hundred years.

Seeing me, she smiles. "Oh good. I'm looking for an angel. It must be you," she says, and continues on her way to post her letters.

I blink and shake my head, taking a while to comprehend I've seen her etheric form, shocked and disoriented by sudden trauma. About to transition to the realms of spirit, her soul had searched for help, literally 'looking for the light'. Because of my meditation minutes earlier, her soul drew her to my high vibrational frequencies for reassurance. She posts more than letters that day.

Jonny, another energy healer, and I spend several hours shepherding hundreds of dazed people wandering the shambolic streets. We calm and direct to relative safety those who are too shocked to think for themselves. Shaken overseas visitors can no longer return to their inner-city hotels, so we find city workers and shoppers willing to take strangers home with them.

High season is in full swing, with thousands of tourists flocking to the garden city, famed for its cultivated beauty and as a gateway to the rugged Southern Alps. Christchurch forefathers established an antipodal slice of England, with weeping willows gracing the banks of a river flowing past handsome stone buildings. It is the perfect place to wear a flat-topped straw hat while punting on the Avon River in a flat-bottomed boat. But over the decades, Christchurch has earned the notoriety of a conservative old boys' network dominating the city's culture and direction.

A plethora of thoughts flap noisily around my mind as Jonny and I walk closer towards the inner-city wreckage. It seems as though a century's worth of thoughts and beliefs trapped in masonry take flight like a released flock of doves rushing up into the air.

But most of our work will be invisible to any onlooker. With uncanny synchronicity, Jonny and I feel the presence of a soul leaving their body at the same time. I sense Quan Yin is shepherding too, as every so often we stop in our tracks and look at each other with an unspoken knowing. Standing among broken bricks and twisted wooden beams, with respectful reverence to the departing, we hold hands and direct our loving intent toward each soul adjusting to the shock of being wrenched from their physical body.

I think back to eleven years ago when a kind stranger stayed with Tim after calling emergency services then watched his soul leave his body. Now, I hold space for strangers in the same way.

We stop to stare at the Basilica, the mother church of the Roman Catholic Diocese of Christchurch and seat of the Bishop of Christchurch. A thick cloud of white dust rises from two collapsed front towers of our country's finest Renaissance building. Strong neoclassical pillars of white stone hold fast, but we can see the huge dome looks unstable. Craning his neck, Jonny exclaims, "Look up there. The statue of Mother Mary. She's turned around!"

Sure enough, the lovely, blue-robed stone figure standing in the north tower, who once faced towards the great church, has rotated 180 degrees. Her arms hold her cloak open, reaching toward the people in the battered city below.

"Wow, that's a powerful statement," I say.

"A symbol of survival?"

"More than that. Mother Mary is declaring her love for all the people. She is shining her light towards them, not the Church."

Standing still to absorb this, another link with Glastonbury comes to mind. "Jonny, all this reminds me of the ransacked churches in England during the Reformation."

"What was that all about?" asks Jonny, tugging his hand from my arm. He yearns to visit Glastonbury and see for himself the stories of my recent experience at the abbey, the Tor, and the Chalice Well gardens.

Collecting my wits, "Here goes. It was an attempt by the ordinary people to weaken the stranglehold of the Church. Inspired by rediscovered humanist principles during the Italian Renaissance, they demanded change. The Renaissance brought so much light to Europe, it frightened the dickens out of the Vatican. It needed to be snuffed out."

Remembering this is no time to climb onto my soapbox, and with a prickling sensation around my head signalling another soul passing, I conclude, "Let's hope humanity never allows the light to be shut down again."

One hundred and eighty-five souls pass into spirit that day. Thousands more suffer serious injuries but, as chance would have it, an international convention had brought six hundred doctors to the city that week. Some even assisted in the extraction of people trapped beneath structures, mitigating damage to limbs.

I've stayed too long. The roads are now gridlocked with anxious drivers. Filled with compassion and more alert than afraid, I see the faces of fellow drivers contort with fear each time aftershocks wobble our cars like shivering jellies. I can't reach Lyttelton that night and stay with Grant, skipper of Grace Lowry. With cell coverage down, I tune in to Laura's energy field and know she is safe. News has already filtered out that this time Lyttelton suffered severe damage.

Morning arrives and, although it's safer to stay in the unaffected outer suburbs, I have an irrational desire to be near my grandchildren. After buying food and water, undeterred by the closed road tunnel that separates us, I negotiate traffic jams again, determined to find an alternative route. Heading out of town toward Sumner, my plan is to drive over the same winding road Tim died on. Swerving past collapsed walls and crumbling hillsides, I reach the summit only to be blocked by a massive rockfall. Standing at the cliff edge, peering beneath low, damp cloud, I see church steeples sitting on the ground like enormous witches' hats. Large blocks of red stone spew over the narrow streets, and huge loading cranes on the wharf stand at odd angles. My heart feels their wrench. Knowing I don't have enough petrol to retrace my steps and approach Lyttelton from the last remaining option of Dyers Pass, I notice an empty parked car. Someone must have legged it down the track. Tired and chilled to the bone, I consider walking these rugged hills too, not knowing how unstable and unsafe they are. With reluctance, I concede my lightweight clothes and high-heeled shoes are not suited to a rugged hike, even without lugging bulky bags of food.

In this moment of near defeat, a shadowy apparition steps through the mist, carrying a bicycle. He tells me of his hair-raising ride up the winding road, dodging and hauling his bike over rockfalls. The day before, his wife was forced to abandon her car here, and he gave his own car to a stranger. With no idea of its whereabouts, he's come to collect this one.

We drive the long way around the hills over Dyers Pass, dismayed to see collapsed houses, overturned cars, and buckled roads. I call him my angel on wheels and hand over some of my provisions. He says there will be a food angel at his family table tonight.

Relieved to find everyone unharmed, I read stories and play games with Aarliah Rose and Harlin. Laura's family will sleep on mattresses under the dining table for many months as relentless aftershocks disrupt their lives. Having started school eight days earlier, along with fifty other small children, Aarliah Rose had been frolicking in a swimming pool when the quake struck. It is a miracle no child drowned when big waves formed in the pool. Her school closes and reopens so many times afterwards that one day she stands with hands on hips and states matter-of-factly, "If I'd known about all this, I wouldn't have bothered starting school!"

I later heard how Laura calmed children and staff at the Lyttelton Kindergarten, where she works part-time. And as each terrified parent arrived to fetch their child, she soothed them too. As buildings came down, Laura rose up into the tower of strength prophesised by Raman years earlier.

FLYING IN THE FACE OF GRIEF — BY ANNWYN

Returning to my cottage later that same day, I open the kitchen door to be greeted by lentils, rice, chickpeas, and smashed glass storage jars. Although the cottage appears sound enough, the two-storey brick and concrete convent next door looks set to topple. Being uphill from my cottage, the cottage will potentially be buried if the convent collapses. A phone call brings Victoria rushing to help, and in ten adrenaline-filled minutes, we clear a path through the debris. We carry my possessions into the driveway, diving out to open space at every violent aftershock. Despite widespread looting, my unattended worldly goods stood untouched for three days and nights. I stay with friends for the first few days and spend my time walking around our small port village, offering energy healing to anybody who wants it. I haven't resided in Lyttelton since.

Quite 'by chance', prior to the quakes, friends had asked me to house-sit their beautiful house and garden in North Canterbury. Removed from the chaos of Christchurch, the peace and beauty of this sanctuary gives me a taste of survivor's guilt. More house-sits follow, and I shift from one beautiful home to another at a time when thousands are without water, electricity, sewerage, or shopping facilities.

Grief floods the streets along with the black liquefaction. I fret about not helping people. In truth, my clients are scattered to the four winds and some never return to the city. From my human perspective, I feel awkward about my good fortune. Yet I understand from a spiritual perspective that my dark night of the soul lies behind me. It is a time for inner celebration of my journey that has transmuted grief into love and despair into joy. Having accomplished this aspect of my inner spiritual growth, I do not need to experience grief again.

CITY OF LIGHT

My fellow citizens, however, are embarking on the very same epic journey I've returned from. Passing them in the transition lounge as we head in opposite directions, I recognise the strain on their faces and hear anxiety in their conversations that include uncommon words such as liquefaction and Richter scale. I feel their hopelessness and understand their roadmaps will be folded and refolded as they suffer the uncertainty that sudden change brings. Their loss contains several layers. Loved ones have perished, and family members moved away. Careers, homes, whole neighbourhoods, and a substantial part of the city has changed beyond recognition — along with their pasts and their futures.

The wake of New Zealand's worst natural disaster triggers a recognition that another chapter of Tim's premature departure now begins — we will work together as messengers of hope. With this realisation comes the clarity that I will write the book Almora spoke of prior to the 2010 pilgrimage. When I'd angled for more details, he didn't divulge further. Following his suggestion, I journalled the pilgrimages to Sweden, Ireland, Cornwall and Somerset, suspecting my book might be about the many otherworldly experiences encountered there. But, under the watchful eyes and wise wings of Tim, the real purpose of the book dawns. Witnessing grief turning people into weeping willows, the trees their beautiful garden city is famous for, I pound the keys with an earnest desire to ease their sorrowful hearts.

At first, human nature shines a bright light through these dark and difficult times. Strangers form friendships, and neighbours rekindle supportive communities. Ten thousand people desert the city, while thousands of new citizens arrive to plan and rebuild it. During this honeymoon period, a unique, unseen energy holds Christchurch within a compassionate embrace. I liken it to the nurtured cradling experienced by Laura and me after Tim passed.

For the first twelve months, stories of heroism and random acts of kindness filled newspapers as the new norm, but good news has a sell-by date. It was time for the juicy stuff.

Culpability enters the city, wearing a folded white cloak embroidered with black detailing. Headlines change from one day to the next, such is the temporary nature of conditional human love. Gaia cannot be held accountable for her shaking body, but someone must.

Crumpling the café's newspaper into a ball with a look of disgust, Laura says, "I can't believe it. Our firefighters, medics, and other emergency rescue staff are being blamed."

"You're kidding. What on earth for?"

"For not doing enough or not doing the correct thing in the first twenty-four hours. They risked their lives for others," she cries, her Gemini emotions rising along with her voice. "Hero to zero. Why do people always have to blame someone?"

Tongue in cheek, unable to resist our role reversal, I say, "Drink your coffee, darling, people are looking."

I agree with Laura's observations. The need to apportion blame is imprinted on the human psyche. I recognise the unfolding process at once — I had treated Manny the same way whenever I couldn't reconcile my angst. We humans are prone to apportion blame both on a personal and collective level, the latter being quick to gain traction.

Over the ensuing months, engineers, architects, builders, doctors, nurses, mayors, and bishops are given roles similar to those portrayed in the latest novel by Hilary Mantel, Wolf Hall. Events parallel Henry VIII's bullying reformation tactics of the Tudor period in England, sullying the reputations of the city's learned men and women. A schism develops between the Bishop of Canterbury and the exemplary Dean of the Christchurch Cathedral, the latter resigning his position. Nobody is strung up on the gallows, but life sentences of judgment, blame, shame, and guilt are given.

It bears a curious resemblance to events five hundred years ago in England and I'm not the only one noting this. A journalist writes a newspaper article pointing out the parallels. To experience a modern version of cathedrals and churches crumbling into heaps of rubble within weeks of recalling a life where this also happened, albeit for different reasons, is unexpected to say the least. I speculate that Glastonbury, known as England's holiest earth, perhaps shares an antipodal spiritual connection with Christchurch.

A year following the quakes, my speculation gains momentum after hearing surprising information. Joining hundreds of others, I squeezed into New Brighton Hall to hear Judy Satori, an internationally renowned channel for spirit, speak in March 2012. Her guides had requested her to share information regarding the Christchurch quakes from a spiritual perspective.

A month earlier, I had attended one of Judy's weekend retreats, making her laugh when confessing my reaction upon hearing her speak light language for the first time. But observing her petite form on stage, her hand habitually brushing aside her long black fringe, this humble woman fills me with inspiration.

Channelling her spirit guides, Judy explains, "Christchurch happens to sit over a very special part of planet Earth, a location which is currently opening as a vortex."

The person seated next to me whispers, "What's a vortex?"

"It's a place on earth where concentrated energy either enters or leaves the earth's plane. Like in the great pyramids of Egypt, and Uluru in Australia, that sort of thing."

Judy goes into greater detail. "The vortex comes direct from the massive crystal at the earth's core." She pauses to receive the next piece of information. When she speaks again, emotion overwhelms her. "And it is this light and energy brought forth by this vortex that, in time, will transform Christchurch into the world's first City of Light."

Murmurations of astonished joy ripple around the hall. I turn in delight to my neighbour, but she has a blank look on her face. "It means Christchurch will become a spiritual centre. Like Glastonbury in England."

"Deep below Christchurch," continues Judy, "is a tectonic plate that rests on two different and unstable types of geological matter. When the energy from the vortex pushes and pulses upwards, it creates movement and friction between the plates, which causes the quakes. It is thought the inner city of Christchurch will be relocated at some point so as not to be further affected by this plate."

People mill around outside the hall after Judy finishes speaking. No one wants to leave — we all want to talk about the revelation of the vortex and the glorious, higher purpose that creates the quakes. People who have lost their homes express how their suffering and loss becomes easier to bear, just as the revelation of Tim's reasons for his departure eased my pain. We regret it will never be reported in a newspaper or believed by most. We see how different people might feel, knowing they lived through an historical event that will eventually bring enormous change to their lives and to the world. There is never a crowd at the leading edge.

Long before the 2010 earthquakes, Almora also spoke in a general way of future changes and challenges facing humanity. He pointed out that tribulations depend on the time in history and whatever issues are relevant to the collective consciousness of that time. In other words, the challenges reflect whatever the imbalances are that humanity needs to work on.

He said, "During different times in history, there have been different things to overcome. At the beginning of this century, challenges of war and famine, poverty and unemployment dominated people's lives. Whereas the challenge for humanity of this consciousness is not only the upheaval of Earth changes but also the breaking down of the monetary and financial systems, both of which you've all relied upon for so long."

His prophetic words bear true for Christchurch citizens who will face both of these challenges for many years to follow. Families now search to find food, water, sanitation, shelter, and income — all the things they enjoyed and took for granted in a developed country. Ten thousand houses will be rebuilt, but 3,500 are demolished. On top of that, insurance companies refuse to cover damages to properties. Many families endure financial struggles, paying mortgages for homes they can't live in while also paying for rented accommodation. As businesses become untenable, job losses occur, forcing Christchurch into a local financial reset.

My journey of grief was a necessary initiation for me to become a beacon of light. Now, an entire city grapples with its opportunity to follow the same pathway into expanded consciousness through a healed, compassionate heart. If Christchurch is indeed destined to be a City of Light, its occupants will need to raise their consciousness. In doing so, they blaze a trail for other cities around the globe going through the same transition. Foretold by ascended masters, humanity has entered a phase of spiritual upgrade.

Chapter 18

SACRED CLOSURE

*'I tend to my mother as though a newborn.
This tender act, a reversal of roles,
brings profound closure to our shared cycle of life.'*

My aged mother lives conflicted. Afraid to live and afraid to die. Several months after my pilgrimage to Glastonbury, her periodic bouts of depression worsen. During our frequent telephone conversations, I yearn to share my insights about the nature of our eternal soul with her. But just as Corky blocked my emotional healing, her orthodox Christian beliefs block hers.

Her frail voice wobbles down the end of the phone, "I'm being punished."

"What do you mean, Mum?"

"The minister doesn't visit anymore."

"Oh, Mum. Why do you think this is punishment?"

"I've been divorced. Twice. I'm nearing the end of my life, and God is angry with me."

Since moving to a rest home a year ago, these daily thoughts torment her. My heart goes out to her and, after making inquiries, I discover her address hasn't been updated. Pastoral visits resumed and, although somewhat consoled, she still fears dying. Mindful and respectful of what she's able to receive owing to her personal beliefs, I keep the lid on mine. But I know the mere fact of talking about her impending death brings some comfort. One day she reveals her greatest fear - falling and suffering a lonely, painful death. She reads in the newspaper about aged people undiscovered for days, weeks. Even worse in her mind, to become terminally ill and die a slow death in hospital. Searching for a way to ease her mind, I broach the subject in a different way.

Speaking with extra softness, I say, "Are you ready to let go of your life, Mum?"

She pauses, then says in her small, thin voice, "Yes. I'm tired."

With that established, over the following weeks, I gently seed an idea I hope will help. "Mum, did you know we all choose the moment of our birth?"

"No. I didn't know that." A slight rise in her voice indicates curiosity, encouraging me to continue.

"And you know, we also choose the moment of our death," I hold my breath. The line crackles.

"Is that so?"

"If you could choose, how would you like to pass to the next world?" She remains silent. I provide cues. "Perhaps while dozing in your favourite chair, or maybe slipping away in your sleep?"

SACRED CLOSURE

She gives her hoarse little laugh, "Slipping away in my sleep. I suppose."

"Alright. Then let Jesus know that's what you'd like to do."

"Alright," she sniffs, "I will. Goodbye dear. I love you."

I cry after she ends the call. I haven't heard those words very often during our journey together.

Several weeks later, I have a nagging sense I must ring her. Busily baking for visitors, I decide I will call her later that day. My guests stop buttering their second helping of cheese scones when Laurie, my eldest brother, rings. He tells me Mum suffered a major stroke in the early hours of the morning. She now lies in hospital, unconscious with a huge brain bleed and is not expected to recover.

"When did staff find her?" I want to know, annoyed at myself for ignoring the earlier prompts to call her.

"They noticed her missing from the dining room at lunchtime."

I sigh with relief, "At least she wasn't alone for long."

"Can you come?"

"I'll be on the next flight."

Aghast at finding a television set blaring in Mum's small room, I hold my tongue. My family doesn't share my concept of the sacredness of death. I can see how upset they are. Familiar background noise feels better than a hanging silence in the room.

Mum lies on her side, her frail body draped in white hospital sheets. Her eyes are closed. She wears an oxygen mask on her face, and I notice the elastic strap pulling on her ears.

FLYING IN THE FACE OF GRIEF　　　BY ANNWYN

Tears fill my eyes as I register the fragility of this woman who had birthed five babies within four years - three boys and twin girls. I doubt she ever saw herself as courageous, yet she made the radical decision to shoulder the responsibility of raising us alone. It was uncommon to divorce one's husband in New Zealand in the sixties, deemed socially taboo, unsupported by welfare and frowned upon by the Church. An unsung heroine, my mother suffered terrible shame for the remainder of her days.

Watching her body shudder with the effort of bringing each breath into her lungs, I know she can't stay with us much longer. Bending over, I whisper in her ear, "Don't worry, Mum. Don't worry about anything at all. Just let go. Of everything."

Laurie holds one hand. On the opposite side of the bed, I hold the other. Her eldest son and daughter tending her last hours. Laurie repeatedly asks her to wait for our three siblings who won't arrive until the next day, but I sense she wants to depart.

With nothing else to be done for her, I fuss over her mask strap, tweaking it this way and that. I want to do something tangible for her, then remember to hold her in my heart. I feel Tim's beautiful energy straight away. Encouraged and strengthened, I guessed he too is holding his grandmother in love. She can't respond, but I know she will feel the love in the room.

Sensing her readiness to leave, I ask to have a few minutes with Mum alone. Laurie's family is surprised, but leaves the room. In deep meditation, I ask Mum's guides, angels, and loved ones in spirit to guide her journey to her next realm. Then, stretching over the bed rails, I edge as close as I can.

"Thank you for being my mother. I understand the roles we both played. I love you, and I hope you have the courage to slip away as soon as you wish. You don't have to wait for anybody. It's your sacred choice. Grandma and Grandad are here. Tim is here too. To take you home."

Laurie returns to the room by himself and together we sit with our mother. Within a brief time, her gasping breathing calms into elongated slow in-breaths and out-breaths, with extended pauses between. Her body completely relaxes. Her breathing pattern echoes exercises I do while meditating, like an ancient technique used to access the Otherworld. It strikes me we are always just one breath away from the stillness we call death.

Mum simply stays in silence and stillness. The in-between breath.

She slips away with peaceful ease into the outstretched arms of her spirit family. I will always remember the serenity in her face.

Tim had gifted so much wisdom that not even the death of my mother feels sorrowful. If only my siblings were aware of the incredible love that surrounds them. Perhaps it would lessen their struggles with any regrets or unfinished business.

Another beautiful opportunity to honour my mother comes at the suggestion of the undertaker who asks if I'd like to assist. Helped by this kind woman, I tend to my mother, treating her as though a newborn. This tender act of nurture and reversal of roles brings profound closure to our shared cycle of life. We apply a little makeup and style her hair, and only after smoothing down her best dress with my hands do I notice the absence of knickers. I think it a giggle, but Laurie, waiting in the foyer for me, is scandalised by this oversight and rushes off to find a pair.

Laurie drives us back to my mother's unit at the rest home where the sight of my siblings emptying her possessions onto a truck stuns me. Without a mention to me, the other four had arranged this between themselves. In a split second of soul memory, I recognise the energy of the Abbott of Glastonbury and the ransacking of his monastery while detained in a mock trial. This bizarre moment of betrayal shakes me for a moment—but I let it go.

Over the next few days, I watch my siblings manage their feelings and thoughts. A vast contrast lies between their experience and mine — and they probably think me a cold fish. Apart from a film of moistness about my eyes from time to time, I shed no tears. Far from feeling their intense grief, jubilation that Mum has gone home to the realms of spirit makes it difficult to contain my joy!

When the cars draw away from the crematorium, I look up to see a hawk circling above us. Drawing this to my siblings' attention, they scan the sky for a moment, but none can see it.

They say, "We don't get hawks around here."

Chapter 19

DROPPING OUT

*'Not to shut the door on grief,
but to open the heart to it.
That is my message.'*

Floyd Walker - 2011

A sphere of shimmering violet-blue light hovers in my inner mind again. Sometimes this orb creates a gentle pulse in the centre of my forehead; other times, it floats about the room like an iridescent balloon. After several weeks, I note how I often think of Floyd when the orb appears. This close friend of Tim and Laura's had taken his life three months before Tim's accident.

Having connected the blue orb with Floyd, over the following weeks my attention is drawn to several magazine articles and television programs about youth suicide. At last, the final puzzle piece arrives - a vivid reenactment of my last encounter with Floyd plays out in my mind's eye.

FLYING IN THE FACE OF GRIEF   **BY ANNWYN**

It's late and I'm driving up Canterbury Street in Lyttelton after an evening with friends. Streetlights are few, but my headlights reveal a dark figure weaving across the road. Slowing down as I drive closer, I recognise Floyd. Dressed in an oversized hoodie, he wears baggy trousers with the crotch almost to his knees. He's a forlorn figure, drinking from a bottle concealed in a brown paper bag. I watch him stagger and sway in the middle of the road, knowing he could easily be one of my children.

Pulling alongside, I lower my window to greet him. "Hi Floyd. Are you okay?"

He focuses his eyes and gives me a cheeky grin. "Hi Tim's mum. Yeah, I'm good."

"Hop in, love. I'll take you home?"

"Nah." The booze makes him smile again. "Thank you, but I'll walk."

"You sure, mate? It's no trouble."

"Yeah. I'm fine."

"Okay." I'm dubious. "Take care, Floyd."

"You, too. Good night, Tim's mum."

Floyd hung himself in a churchyard one week later.

His death shocks Tim and Laura to their core. I feel terrible guilt for not having done more that night. Despite living in a small, village-like community where people care about each other, and despite our community initiative to employ a full-time youth worker, we lost many teens right under our noses. In fact, I am a founding member and past president of the Lyttelton Youth Council, established to support teens at risk exactly like Floyd.

This last encounter with Floyd plays repeatedly, vivid and lifelike. Although I don't understand it, I decide to meditate on the blue orb to see what might unfold. The orb speaks loud and clear, transmitting feelings of shame and self-blame. In a flash, I get it. This message relates to the guilt, stigma, and social taboo associated with suicide. The moment I understand this, the orb transmits palpable joy!

Apologising to the orb for being so thick, I sit contemplating the double standard between accidents and suicide. I know Floyd's parents suffer agonising regrets of 'if only'. I had done this myself at first — 'if only' I had stayed home with Tim that day. But I now understand accidents and illnesses are ways in which souls return to the spirit realms through conscious soul choice.

My thoughts roll back to Laura's terrified cry for help in the bath that day, and I recall my own vulnerability. Her desperate act had forced me to face the frailty of my own reason to live. Several times I too had entertained dark notions such as driving off a steep and windy road — there were plenty around the volcanic hills of Lyttelton to choose from. At that time, Laura was my sole basis for remaining on the planet and had she left, my reason for living would have gone with her.

Anticipating these shadows of grief, my soul had swung into action, sowing the seeds of curiosity I would feel compelled to investigate. Within hours of Tim's death, during the drive home it had whispered tantalising prompts to remind me of our soul family arrangements. Having planted paradoxical excitement amidst sorrow, it steered me towards a chain of individuals, messengers Geraldine and Ishtar, who led me to the enlightened teachings of Raman concerning the eternal soul.

Under Raman's tutelage, my desire to depart turned toward a desire to stay. I needed a strong rationale to stay, should Laura succumb to her shadowy depths. I had stood on shaky ground at that period, because my life purpose hinged upon others.

Flipping back to Floyd, I step into his bewildered shoes — size seventeen years, with pointy toes. Remembering Laura's curiosity about Floyd I hunt out a dusty cassette tape of Raman from eleven years ago and settle on the couch to listen through a different set of ears.

First of all, Laura wants to know if Floyd and Tim are together.

Knowing her fondness for him, Raman smiles and then answers her question in loving detail. "They have met and embraced each other — they are very pleased to see each other. Very pleased indeed."

He continues, "And I can say Floyd has forgiven himself. You see, he had a lot of regrets, a lot of regrets. He was not in a good space when he left; he was not happy. He believes he tried to let others know, but at the end of the day, he also felt quite ashamed — that he had, as he calls it, 'mucked up'. Now, he is on a little bit of a treadmill, difficult to get off unless someone stands in front of him and says, 'Stop!' Deep down, he hopes someone will do that. But of course, that would be hard to do around him, would it not?

I want you to know he was afraid he would be in trouble. But there is no sin to this; he is not being punished. He has simply woken up and has received a lot of counsel, of healing. He is in a much better space."

Laura nods, taking this all in, and asks, "Is there a reason why he killed himself?"

"Dear heart, he found it difficult to handle how he felt about himself. He had quite a battle with himself and with his choices. He knew he kept avoiding things that he needed to do. Every time he looked at himself, he found that he didn't like what he saw. Then he had to put a lot of energy into the facade, you know the one, being happy, letting everyone know that he was all right. Play acting, but that really wasn't him. He hoped someone would watch and say, 'That's not you…what are you doing?'"

I hand Laura my tissues after wiping the corners of my eyes.

Speaking directly to Laura, he says, "I also want you to realise, because you are a part of this, dear one, that for the young generation incarnated now, it is a very difficult period. And some do fall through the cracks. Simply because, and you may tell me if I am wrong, you find it hard to relate to the old. You don't know where you fit, and you know you've come to be different, but the future is not formed yet.

"I want to remind you gently and lovingly; you are here for a reason — you are here for your own learning — but you are also here because you are a member of a new generation that has come to make a difference.

"Of course, you will look around and see much that is wrong with this world, and there is quite a lot wrong, so you're not going to feel happy about it. You don't want to be part of it; you don't want to perpetuate it. You will look at the pollution, the wars, the demands and cultural expectations in your society. And you will say, 'I don't fit', 'I don't want to be a part of it'. But it is also important for you to look and notice all that is sustainable and beautiful. For the things that endure through their innate wisdom and beauty have the potential to be developed by following generations. If you only see the negative, if you focus on that, then that will become your reality, dear one."

He pauses to allow Laura to absorb his message. She turns to me with a look that says, "It's a wonder any of us stay."

"So, remember, dear heart, that you are allowed to look for joy! To be happy, to make your life work. You don't have to hold yourself back just because your brother cannot be with you. You must not sacrifice yourself. It is his greatest concern, dear heart, that you will sabotage yourself and your life because he has left. But this was his soul's choice. This is a choice you must allow yourself to face. And to know that as you face it, you have a mother who loves you very much — I love you very much — and you can have all the support in the world. It is important for you not to hold in how you feel. Even when you feel you shouldn't say these things, let them out, dear heart. So that you can hear them and, also, so that others can hear them and can help you."

Laura sniffs, wanting to hear more about her friend. "So Floyd's okay?"

"He is doing very well. And he's receiving advice on how he can resume life. You see, if you opt out before your time, then you are encouraged to come back."

"Was it his time?" she asks.

"Indeed, it was not! He has a lot of potential."

"Can you please send love from his mum and dad and from his sister?"

"Yes, indeed," he beams. "It is my pleasure. He loves them very much, and it causes him enormous distress that he hurt the ones he loves. He has immense guilt about this. It is a great difficulty for him.

"Dear heart, when he died and saw the outpouring of love and grief for him, he realised support really was there for him, but he had been afraid to ask for it. He is afraid that his actions mean that everybody is against him now. He really thinks he has mucked up."

Sharing my own guilt, I say, "I think as a community we have 'mucked up.' That we didn't see or act on what we saw."

"Dear one, it's important to realise it is difficult to see because these little souls are masters at camouflage. And of course, when they put up smoke screens, their parents look at them with concern. They can see what they are doing, but they don't realise it is a call for help. So, you must not blame yourselves but realise these young individual souls are learning and growing. Just like you, they will make individual choices."

At the next session, Laura again inquires after Floyd, asking if our Lyttelton lads have connected again.

"Yes, they have. From a human perspective, they don't see much of each other, but their meetings hold extreme value for both. And of course, Floyd knew from the moment he left this world that your brother would be joining him. So, he anticipated his arrival and has been very loving and supportive of your brother since he arrived.

"But they are different energies and have different things to learn. It is like going to the same school but realising you are choosing different courses. Although you can choose to get together sometimes, a lot of the time you are apart."

"Floyd wasn't religious." Laura frowns. "I don't understand why he chose the churchyard."

"Because, at the moment he went there, he wasn't planning to commit suicide, though of course, everybody thinks he was. He didn't want to create a fuss at home and went there seeking solace and guidance. He turned to the one thing he knew in his heart was the authority of life above all life. And in secret, he was deeply religious."

Raman smiles at the surprise on Laura's face. "He would have kept this to himself. Had he remained, he would have explored spirituality quite strongly. Even though it wasn't fashionable, but as you know, he liked to set trends."

"So, in going there, he was seeking understanding, some solace, and he found two things. One, he discovered that he couldn't reconcile his thoughts, his feelings, and his actions. He had done things he wasn't happy about, and in the face of all that he felt he was not good enough. It reinforced his thought that he was making a mess of his life."

Softening his voice, Raman explains, "The other aspect, when he became quiet and calm, he felt a great presence, a great love, and he desired that over all else. It was the one thing, the one place, and he made a choice."

"But you need to understand his torment. Yet, at the same time, because he moved in and out of these two spaces, he was also very calm and clear about what he planned to do. Choosing the churchyard was his cry for help. It was also a message he wanted to tell his parents, his mother in particular, where he was going and where he wanted to be as an alternative to life."

"Is there a message from Floyd to pass on to his family?" whispers Laura, shaken by these deep insights into her friend.

"He wishes to convey his absolute enjoyment at the efforts being made in the garden. I believe there is a particular memorial. He wishes to convey his awareness of this development and give his approval. It is a significant and important thing. He encourages them to continue their garden development because he wants to be a part of things that are living and growing. He is pleased to be remembered in this way.

"He wishes to let his family know that he visits often. He sits in his usual place at an odd angle when they gather in the living room; he still takes his place. He's often amused that no one knows he's there. He doesn't like to intrude too much; he still feels uncomfortable about hurting his family. And therefore, he's not as confident as your brother is about coming and letting everybody know he's there! He will learn to do this as he heals. He is still working through his own grief and guilt.

"He doesn't want his father to feel guilty. I see that his father torments himself with not knowing — that he should have seen. Floyd hid it well. There was nothing his father could have seen, nor was there anything he could have said that would have made a difference. It was not about his father. If you would convey this, Floyd would be delighted. There's a lot of healing needed in his family now."

Listening to this incredible information, I'm eager to find out more about the blue orb, but wait until my next session with Almora, and also ask Floyd's permission to use his story.

Through Almora, Floyd gives his immediate approval with the words, "Yes, indeed, a privilege."

I ask if Floyd would like to contribute his own message about death and grief. He begins, slow at first, then gathers confidence.

"There is no separation between life and death. There is no fear in dying. I am able to see and do more from where I am now at this time than if I'd stayed. And through the experience of life and death, there are many gifts to be gained, if you are able to recognise them.

"In recognising the privileges of life, with death immense healing can occur between families and friends that would not have occurred otherwise. For in that death, they can be united in their grief and appreciate each other through the healing process. Sometimes it divides families. Sometimes it divides friends. But it is always an opportunity for them to come together and heal, and appreciate their lives and their journeys, and precious, precious life. Because life is nothing really without those you love. And often in life, that is forgotten until there is death. And then, death itself is not appreciated either.

"So, coming together in grief is a profound clearing and healing process, and it connects every person because every person in this world, at some time, will feel grief."

He adds in closing, "Not to shut the door on grief, but open your heart to it. That is my message."

With my hands over my heart, I thank him. "Your beautiful words will reach so many hearts, bringing much healing. Your contribution is much appreciated. Blessings to your heart."

"Thank you for being the messenger for us and thousands of others —millions of others. This is a very beautiful gift to the world, to all of those who have lost someone they love."

"My love to Shane, Jimmy, Chloe, Jess, Shakira, Georgina." I try to recall the names of young people connected to Tim and Laura who have passed early. Sadly, there are many more.

"And all love to you too."

When our touching, loving conversation finishes, Almora describes the energies in the room.

"These souls have created a beautiful violet-blue orb for their group energy of love, dear one. It floats here between us, glistening in the light."

Visualising this beautiful image, my tears flow and I understand how much these souls want their message heard. "Ooh! I've seen that in my mind's eye! I wondered who that was! So, they are very often with me?"

"Often with you, and guiding you, and feeling your love as well."

"So beautiful."

"Very beautiful. You are a messenger for them, and also for here, dear one. Between the worlds…you walk between the worlds."

Right on cue, within a matter of days, I bump into Floyd's father. Puffing my way up a steep Lyttelton street, it is a good excuse to stop. Catching my breath, I tell him about the blue orb and my communication with his son. He can't believe I have actually talked with Floyd. Amazed, and brimming with tears, he consents to sharing Floyd's story.

"Yes," he says, wiping his eyes with his sleeve, "So that others may learn and heal."

Walking away from Floyd's dad, a bulb lights up. Almora usually relays information from Tim and my other guides, but with Floyd, I had spoken firsthand. Therefore, I can do the same with Tim! Buoyed with excitement, my mountain goat legs effortlessly bound home to book an appointment.

Chapter 20

SPIRIT AND HEART WISDOM

*'There is a need for young people to connect with their spirit
and understand the message of the spirit.
Especially the heart because
the mind creates so much pain and suffering.'*

Tim 2011

Standing back, we scrutinise our festive efforts at decorating our local Lyttelton pub. On the gigantic screen, a movie about Tim plays, pieced together by Laura from a collection of photographs. We giggle over the wording of our playful invitation, 'Celebrating Tim's 10th year in his new job!'

"Amazing cake, Mumsy." Laura places the huge heart-shaped chocolate cake centre stage on the table and licks her fingers. "Do you think anyone will come?"

"Maybe they'll think it's bizarre. Not everyone sees things the way we do, love. Ten years in his new job. What were we thinking?"

FLYING IN THE FACE OF GRIEF   **BY ANNWYN**

"You wanna know something?" says Laura, mischief dancing over her beautiful face. A hint of chocolate smears the corner of her mouth. Couldn't wait for the party to begin. "Who cares and so what!"

Laura, 'flying in the face of grief.'

Fifty people turn up. Laura's two children steal the show, their mother glowing each time someone declares, "My, this little one looks like his uncle." Indeed, two-year-old Harlin looks very much like Tim. Four-year-old Aarliah, confident and curly-headed, twirls to her uncle's favourite music in her pink dress and sparkly shoes.

Friends boogie and take turns at the mic, sharing quirky stories that typify the Tim they remember. Now in their late twenties, they laugh throughout a short homemade skateboarding movie that captures teenage antics of 'down trousers' and smoking forbidden cigarettes on camera. Ra, looking dapper in his own men's designer clothing label delivers a heart-warming speech.

After everyone leaves, Laura and I collapse on a sofa. Tired and happy, we talk about the party and sip one last glass of wine. "This was such a good idea, Mum."

"I can't believe how much everyone wanted to share their stories and their feelings. A lot of healing happened tonight, sweetie."

"Yeah. Remember how they were at the funeral?"

"I do. Broken-hearted, bewildered teenagers."

"I think Tim would be blown away."

"You know what they loved most? Seeing your children. Knowing you have survived."

"Really?" She sniffs, her eyes welling up.

"Absolutely. I believe that seeing your happiness gives them permission to bring closure to their own grief."

"Well, something good happened then. They all want to do it again in another five years!"

"Amazing! Although I struggled to stop myself from standing up and banging a spoon against a glass. I wanted to share what he's doing. But that wouldn't have gone down well."

Laura blows her nose and chuckles. "Like, oh Tim's helping young people settle back into the spirit realms after they arrive distressed?"

"Even better, imagine if we tell them Tim's probably going to reincarnate quickly back into our family, but into a different culture." We laugh, sharing what only we can share.

"It is a shame that we can't tell them about his incredible work. And that he will return to help people through their ascension."

"Yeah. They'd think we've lost the plot."

We grin at each other, clink our glasses, and shout, "Who cares and so what!"

Almora later confirmed Tim very much appreciated the celebration and gave more details about Tim's service in the spirit realms. "Part of his work is with young people who have incarnated and struggle to stay on Earth. Like young Floyd, the world is too difficult for them. Often these are 'the sensitives'. These children are very evolved souls, vibrating at high frequencies of love and compassion. This makes them vulnerable in the world of dense, low-frequency thoughts, words and actions. Tim has studied and developed the ability to come to them in dream state. In this way, he encourages and supports them, and they remember their dreams on awakening."

"Oh, that is wonderful work," I say, "These 'new' children need that support."

"Yes, dear heart. And at some point in the future, you will work together. He from his realm, and you from yours. Together you will encourage these unique and gifted children. Also their parents, who often experience great challenges as the parents of these sensitive children who arrive with higher consciousness."

"That's exciting. How wonderful that would be."

Changing the topic, I make the request that has motivated this session. "Almora, I want to ask if it's possible for me to converse directly with Tim? I feel compelled to speak to him about his experiences before, during, and after the accident. It seems to me we focus on the ones left behind and often don't consider how it is for the departed, simply because we believe their life has ended. In doing so, we neglect to honour and recognise their spirit life. Well, usually, that is." I smile, recalling our recent party.

Almora sounds delighted by this idea. "This is your awareness speaking and is unique. It comes from you, from within you. That is your creative process, and it is a very good thing to do.

"I invite you to call in your beloved son now. I am most happy to facilitate, but I believe the connection needs to be from you, rather than from me, so I will sit and hold the energy, the space."

"Will I hear him?" I'm worried my nervousness will act as a block.

"Ah, well, first spend a moment here with me, before meeting him in a sacred space. Have you got a sacred space where you go in your meditations, like a temple or garden?"

"No, not a special space." I gazed at the ceiling for inspiration. "Let's go to the Chalice Well gardens in Glastonbury."

"Very well. Close your eyes and breathe. When you connect with the beating of your heart, you connect with the universal life force that is you. You enter into the openness of all of life. As your heart beats, you are reminded love is what you are, and love is what created you. Now see yourself entering the gardens at the Chalice Well at nightfall under a full moon. Nobody else is there in this peaceful, ancient and sacred land. Make your way over moonlit flagstones, through the arched gateway, and sit by the water - the place where he came to you once before."

"In 2010, on the steps of King Arthur's Court? After recalling my lifetime as the Glastonbury Abbot?"

"Yes, dear one. The place where he came to you for the last time in his human role as your son."

"I remember. I have a sense of his growth, Raman. He feels magnificent."

"Indeed. Invite him now to come and sit with you."

FLYING IN THE FACE OF GRIEF   **BY ANNWYN**

"Beloved Timothy, I would be honoured and grateful if you would join me and commune for a while. If this is your heart's desire, my intention is to offer you the opportunity to talk about your time just preceding your departure, the departure itself, and after the departure. But only if this feels comfortable and you are willing. I believe it may be extremely useful for humanity at this time. Blessings to your heart, dear one."

Almora instructs, "Open your heart to his energy, dear one, ask him to sit with you, join in your company."

"Please sit with me by these sacred waters in King Arthur's Court," I murmur, already in a deep meditative state.

Almora opens the circle, "We create a space of love, a space of openness and trust." He adds, "What are you aware of, beloved one?"

"I see and feel the beautiful red energy that I know to be Tim's energy. I feel very peaceful, very loved."

"Indeed. So now we go back, dear one, to the year prior to the accident, 1999. Just let yourself remember the things going on in his life, what it felt like, what you noticed."

"A lot of trauma. Tim suffered a psychotic episode. He recovered from that really well after an amazing amount of work. He worked at the Lyttelton Marina, moving into his manhood. He made a big effort to reconnect with his father. Laura lived at Mount Cook at the time.

We shared a house together, enjoying each other's company. A friendship, rather than mother and son at that stage."

Without noticing the subtle slipstream of transition, I'm now speaking with Tim. "And I remember, just sometime before the accident in 2000, you became very distressed about Jessica and Floyd taking their lives. You felt they were calling you, and we thought you were relapsing into another psychotic episode. Do you remember that, dear one?"

"Yes," Tim answers through Almora's voice.

"What did it feel like?"

"As a confusing time because it felt so real that it became difficult to discern between dreams and reality. And which reality represented my truth, my true life, and where I needed to be. And I became more and more disconnected from life here, and the world here. It started to feel overwhelming, very loud. While the feeling I got from being in the other world was so beautiful, so expanded, so light, and so free. Free of pressure, no demands, no expectations. I felt at home, and I felt accepted."

"Were you consciously thinking about departing? Or were you just conscious that you felt more connected to somewhere else?"

"I felt more connected to being somewhere else.

But I did feel maybe my life there was not going to be a long one."

"Yes, somehow, I knew that too. I often sensed in my dream state that I would lose you. At different times, I saw a car going into the water. And when you departed I gradually remembered these events were meant to be, eventually understanding our preordained agreement, and that we would all be okay. And I entered a curious state of grace about it, without knowing where that came from."

"And it became a healing for family and friends and other people. Because I made everybody else look differently at life."

"Tim, you gave so much. Your leaving – I honour the gifts held within this supreme sacrifice. So much happens now that wouldn't have happened. The paradox is how much I love you and would love to have you here. But I also acknowledge and honour what we have with you being in another dimension."

"And I love you very much. It wasn't easy."

"I understand your dilemma."

"One foot in each camp, in each place."

"How long did you feel like that, dear one?"

"About two years."

This piece of information shocks me. "Oh! My goodness, such suffering. Is there anything you could say to other young people who might feel the same?"

"In human form, there is a need for them to connect with their spirit and understand the message of the spirit, especially the heart, because the mind creates so much pain and suffering. People think they know what you need and what is right for you. Many think you have mental illness. But mental illness is really just another state of consciousness."

"I know, and as your mother, I ask your forgiveness for admitting you to hospital. For failing to recognise the meaning of those unfolding events at the time."

"I receive that with love, dear mother, but I never blamed you for that. You did the best you could to take me under your wing."

"How would you reach somebody at that age?

"Through music, through writing, through other young people because that's who they listen to. And there are young people now who are wise teachers, planted in schools and youth clubs, and sports clubs. They are there to bring that wisdom and that light and plant those seeds. They are the ones who will help lead the way."

"Like our dear Harlin and Aarliah-Rose?"

"Yes. And through awareness, they teach the mothers and fathers how to parent their children differently. To know that these children are the sensitives. The parents will need to learn about feelings, creativity, uniqueness, diversity, and resist putting the children into categories. Not create competition through intellect, through sports, through clothes, but to celebrate the uniqueness of all the different expressions. If they are given that opportunity, their children will flourish and be the best of who they are. They are the future teachers, physicians, politicians, spiritual teachers, nutritionists, musicians. In this way they will create a new way of living in the world.

"What memory do you have of your death?"

"It all happened very fast, and I remember thinking that my life was coming to an end. I didn't know when, but I felt it. I started to remember all the different things that happened in my life with my father, my mother, my sibling, my friends, my teachers."

"As you were driving down the winding road towards Sumner?"

"Yes, yes, yes. And then, of course, there was the impact and shock. And for a while, I didn't know where I was. I stood in a place of between, looking at my car, seeing myself. Thinking I was dreaming and trying to get back, but not able to."

"You were on your own at that point?"

"Yes."

"Were you frightened?"

"Very frightened during that lonely time. I couldn't get back into my body and I didn't know if I wanted to. I didn't know where I'd landed. And it took a while before I started to see a light. Then the light came, and we sat for a while by the car."

"Who were you with then?"

"A beautiful Māori woman, who called herself Moana. She came from these parts and stayed as a guardian spirit of the land. She watched me driving down the hill and saw the crash. She explained she would sit here with me for a while until someone else came."

"Blessings to you, Moana!"

"Indeed. But did I know where I was and what had happened? At first, I thought I must be dreaming. I didn't know who Moana was, or even what she was, dressed in old clothes I had never seen before." He pauses for a moment. "So, I asked for someone I know. And some of my departed friends came."

"Who came, Tim?"

"My friends, the ones who departed a few months before me. But they didn't look the same, and they used different names."

"Was it Floyd and Jessica?"

"Yes, yes. But they were so different - so happy. They were so full of light - it was hard to believe it was them."

"Ah, that is good to know!"

"Yes, yes. Then, another Being arrived, radiating extraordinary bright light. This Angelic Being asked if I felt ready to go now. Up to a place of healing, a place of transition, a place to review, and to see what had happened. I moved very fast to that place. Almost like moving up very fast in an elevator. It was amazing to finally realise my lightness."

Feeling my emotion, Tim waits for me to settle. "And then, I went to a beautiful place - the only thing I can compare it to is like a beautiful hospital in beautiful gardens - except it wasn't a hospital. There were many rooms with people in them coming and going. It was very peaceful, and nobody spoke except through thought. The minute I thought something, an immediate reply came. I seemed to sleep for a very long time - I'm unsure whether in your time it was three or four weeks or months, even longer.

"After my body healed, I moved to another place to observe my life. This enabled me to remember my life before and to see us both in that life. And even our soul group meeting when we decided to meet again, and what we would all to do together in this life. Including accepting my role in this life."

"So, our family members decided you would leave early?"

"Yes, although I always had choice. It required quite a big evolutionary leap of faith. I'm not sure how to describe it because it's not failure or disappointment. You see, from where I am now, I would like to have made that leap. But after the psychosis, my body was tired, my mind was tired, and my heart was heavy. So, I chose to depart and evolve from the realm of spirit instead."

"And perhaps, with more awareness from myself and from others... I'm not blaming myself, but recognising it would be different now, ten years on."

"Yes. But I could always choose - although I didn't realise it then."

"It's often the way. And you were so young."

"Yes. So that took a lot of healing. I found that hard to remember, and to see the outcome. Since then, I hold great peace in my heart my departure was not in vain."

"Not at all, not at all. And there is more to come!"

"Yes, yes. Now I'm working from spirit to support other young men and women that feel similar. I have an ability to come into their dreams, and they know me in their dream state. In those dreams, they have moments of awareness and memory."

"Beautiful work! I deeply honour your work."

"I receive that, dear beloved. You will always be my mother, and I am privileged to have this time and other times before with you. We journey together many times."

"Do you miss Laura?"

"I do."

"That must have been difficult leaving her behind."

"Yes, yes. I do visit her. Sometimes she feels me, but then gets sad. I would like her to feel love in those moments, not sadness, to know that we are never separated from the ones we love. Is there anything else you would like to ask, dear mother?"

"For now, I am content with our conversation. And I'm very grateful to you for revisiting that painful time and allowing me to bring this to others and expand their understanding. This is a great gift from you, my dear son. It is much appreciated."

"And I send you love and appreciation, dear mother, as a messenger of this beautiful awareness and healing to the many that suffer at this time. More than ever, this is needed. I embrace you in love, mother dear."

"My blessings to your heart. Goodbye for now."

"Peace and Love."

Chapter 21

MY EVER BEING LIFE

*'My life is not cut short.
There are no endings.
I am the Ever Being of Life.'*

Tim

Hanging on every word, I could have talked with Tim forever. But I feel Almora's gentle guidance already steering me back into my body.

"When you are ready, beloved one, make your way out of the Chalice Garden. Give your thanks and appreciation for what you've received, and for the love and healing that took place."

Needing time to reorientate, I realise how far I've travelled in consciousness. "And much gratitude to you too, Almora," I whisper. Overcome with emotion, I bow my head in deep appreciation.

Placing his hands in prayer position, he replies, "It is a great pleasure and privilege to do this work, dear one."

"I know this is going to help many people."

"It will. As you will see, many young people are disconnected from their peers and from their families. And sadly, they are looked upon as being hopeless, dropouts, and failures."

Later that day, Laura wants all the details, enthralled to learn of the lifetime Tim and I shared prior to this one.

"I've sort of known about this for a while. Remember I used to get a sudden stab of sharp pain to the right side of my chest? I attributed it to karmic energy, not a physical thing. So, I asked Almora about it."

"It's Tim prodding you?"

"Yes, sharp prods. We were American Indian sons of a chief, engaged in a battle in 1842 somewhere in North America. To his dismay, Tim killed me with an arrow shot to that exact spot."

"So why poke you there now?"

"Because he suffered terrible guilt and grief which he brought into this lifetime. This is what happens with our unresolved events. We carry them into the next incarnation. He didn't have the chance to resolve it, so he asked for my forgiveness through Almora."

"That's how he gets your attention?"

"Yes, and now it's his signal for me to pay attention to something." Massaging the old wound I add, "I hope he comes up with another way. It hurts."

"Sounds like his humour," she says with a laugh. "Pay back for making him eat spinach."

"Ha! Maybe. According to Almora, that previous Indian lifetime in part shaped the roles we both play in this life." My brow furrows as I say. "I haven't worked that out yet."

Musing during the drive home, I wonder if Tim and I take turns at being embodied or disembodied. I had returned to the realms in our previous life together; this time he took that role. However it works, this long-established pattern of interdimensional collaboration had spared me from the soul trauma suffered by Laura. My challenge had revolved around allowing the deep pain in my heart to heal from previous incarnations, the same pain Tim's death triggered, and that Corky attempted to bury. If not for Manny, I would have joined the walking wounded for the rest of my life, my sorrows dulled through alcohol, drugs, work, sex – the addictions and distractions used by those who never heal.

Nearing her third decade, and a magnet to children and animals, Laura continues to develop aspects of the blueprint foreseen by Raman fifteen years earlier. Lyttelton locals often praised her high-spirited yet practical approach to life in general. She has a knack for getting things done, such as attracting sponsorship for community projects. Her enthusiasm for sport spreads to coaching the junior rugby and netball teams who look smart in their brand-new uniforms thanks to her.

Parenting two strong-willed, high-vibrational children both uplifts and challenges her with their new way of being in the world. Six-year-old Aarliah Rose sings and dances her way through each day, inventing a tune and lyrics for even the most mundane occasion. Sparkling like a gemstone, she gathers her own collection of crystals and often comments on people's auras – that is until, having noticed other people don't talk about such things, she and her sighted friends decide not to mention this anymore.

Like Manny, she possesses an inbuilt bullshit detector. Aged around four years old, she happened to be present when a boyfriend of mine proffered lame excuses for not keeping an arrangement. We were standing outdoors in the sun, Aarliah Rose leaning against the house on one leg, with one foot pressed against the wall. During a natural pause in the conversation, her sing-song voice broke the silence with, "Someone's not telling the truth."

Curly-headed, brown-eyed Harlin looks more like Tim as each month passes. At three and a half years old, he appears a more robust version of his uncle, not quite so sensitive, but as determined as his mother. Harlin once taught me a valuable lesson when sweeping autumn leaves with a yard broom twice his height. Tripping on a concrete step and grazing his leg, he objected when I fussed and poured out a stream of empathy. He allowed me to tend his graze with a band-aid but forbade me to experience his emotions vicariously. The moment my mouth moved to express empathy, he bawled at me to stop. This happened several times until I understood that each act of lowering my vibrational frequencies to match his, amplified what he already felt. He didn't need my misery heaped on top of his own. With that simple act, he taught me neutral compassion.

Seated on my lap one day, he says, "Nanny, your teeth are purple."

Like his sister, he notices auric fields, in this case, the blue purple colour of my throat chakra.

Laura and I still wonder if Tim has indeed reincarnated as Harlin and, during a chat with Almora, I put our query to him.

"He feels familiar to you because he and Tim are twin flames, dear heart."

"But I thought Tim and Laura were twin flames."

"Indeed, they are. Understand that twin flames are created when a soul expands into two. It is common to have many twin flames, but less common for them to incarnate together. Your son and daughter are unique in that way."

He continues with a twinkle in his eye. "You may be surprised to learn, dear heart, that in the original plan, Tim and Harlin were to birth as your twin sons."

"Oh! Then Laura would still have a brother."

"Indeed. But on review, it was decided that to provide greater development of her own self, Harlin would be her son instead. Thus, enabling Harlin to carry on Tim's energy and support her in this way. She is doing so well."

Laura's rocky road had paved the way, leading her to the inner strength her soul had requested in this lifetime. Her partner hauls her over many karmic stones, which she bears with fortitude while observers shake their puzzled heads. The karmic magnet keeps her by his side until the energies rebalance from her unkind treatment of Jason over several lifetimes. After years of standing by him and forgiving his shortcomings, they can now go forward in a smoother relationship, providing they adapt to their new dynamics. Like Manny and me.

Laura often struggles with information I share with her. But she remains open-minded and, over the years, shows increasing awareness of her own messages from spirit. One day around Christmas time, always a challenging time of year for her, I take care of the children and send her off for a long beach walk. An hour or so later, she returns, her face radiant with excitement.

FLYING IN THE FACE OF GRIEF **BY ANNWYN**

"Mumsy, listen to this. I sat down on a bench for a while. I decided to forgive Tim for leaving me. And then I also forgave four of my closest friends who left. When I looked up, I saw five seagulls flying in a circle above me!"

Tears well up and I throw my arms around her. The children whoop and jig about, feeling our joy. "Darling, I'm so proud of you!"

The kids wrap their arms around our legs, saying they are 'pwoud of mummy, too', giggling and enjoying the moment.

"Oh, sweetheart. Imagine the jubilation in the spirit realms. You opened the door! And one day, you will walk through that door to meet Tim without tears."

"Can we have ice cream?" asks Aarliah Rose, showing all her small milky white teeth.

"Yes!" chorus her mother and grandmother.

Licking chocolate drips around the edges of my cone, I wink at Laura. This reluctant soul who likes to take her time to savour. She forgives her brother eleven years later for what she experienced as deep betrayal -taking a huge leap in consciousness in mere minutes.

Hugging them goodbye and wanting to celebrate Laura's spiritual milestone with Tim, I find her bench of forgiveness at Brighton beach. Kicking my sandals off, I dig my toes into the warm sand and close my eyes against distracting scenes of children running into the water and splashing about. Wind rustles through the dry tussocks, softening joyful shrieks and seagull squawks until they fade into a pleasant hum. With the sun kissing my face, I invite Tim to sit on the bench next to me. Soon, I detect a powerful presence, and a gorgeous magenta colour floods my inner sight. This doesn't feel like Tim's energy field but then I know him by his projected thoughts, although these too hold a different expression.

"Mother dearest, you are noticing another level of expansion in my energy field, something I will explain. For now, let us feel the joy of my sister's inner work, because when a family member expands, it affects us all."

"Ah, of course, you foresaw this."

"For some time. In human terms, at least a year ago. Do you recall the moment in the Chalice Well Gardens after your traumatic recollection of the abbot's death?"

"Like it happened yesterday."

"That heralded a defining moment. Can you imagine how much I wished to comfort you? But to reach the higher planes of consciousness means I could no longer engage with you or Laura in an emotional way. This signalled the final shedding of my human attachment to Earth, because I was confident you were set on your spiritual pathway."

"Are you no longer part of the family?"

"Dear Mother, I will always be your son, but one day we will release even those roles. Don't worry, not until you are ready. I am always with the family in varying degrees, but I no longer experience low-density emotions such as fear, grief, betrayal, anger or shame. But you will always feel my peace, love, and joy!"

"Now I see why I couldn't connect with you at the Chalice Well and through those earlier years of deep processing. I am glad you fly so high!"

"I chose to remain attached until your heart healed, knowing that afterwards, you would also soar because you had freed yourself from so many limiting mental constructs. As you neared this point, we all met on the spiritual plane and agreed it was time, including my sister, who from her higher perspective could see she would also soon reach a turning point. She did that today on this very bench."

FLYING IN THE FACE OF GRIEF — BY ANNWYN

I don't always receive immediate communication from Tim, but within a day or two a response arrives. Many times I wake up with the answer flashing across my inner vision, or a key word sounding in my inner ear. We both love teasing cryptic meanings out of lyrics; a popular song will embed itself in my head until I figure it out. But the first song he used was a no brainer. It related to my earliest work channelling energies on land sites, and after transmitting the vibrational frequencies through light language, I wasn't sure what to do next. It was a lovely setting high on the Banks Peninsula hills and I'd just unpacked a picnic lunch when I heard his instructions in no uncertain terms. My ears were filled with the song 'Hit the Road Jack'. Tim doesn't hesitate to grab whoever can relay a message. Smiling strangers at an airport once walked over to say my son was standing next to me with something to say.

But nothing compares with his vivid first message. Within days of his passing, Tim came to me in dream state. In this otherworldly dream, he grew from infancy to manhood before shapeshifting into a white owl. At the time, I thought he wished to show me how he would look in manhood, something a parent yearns to know. Later, I recognised the catalytic effect that prompted me to remember our soul agreements. That vision never fades. I can still bring every detail into my mind's eye, except now I sense a deeper meaning. Alongside this, I notice his presence more than usual. At first, this creates confusion because his energy field looks and feels so different.

Sitting in conversation with Almora, I decide to begin with a story about Harlin that Laura told me a few days earlier. For no apparent reason, he had burst into enthusiasm about our wonderful world. She said it cracked her up to hear this wee tot exclaim, "What a beautiful day! Look at the sun! Look at the beautiful sky! What a perfect day, Mum!" As Laura relayed the scene, I had immediately felt Tim expressing through Harlin.

"Yes, it was his uncle," says Almora. "You are really feeling the messages, dear one. I invite you to explore this further. Begin by closing your eyes. Notice any little orbs of light in your mind's eye."

He continues, "As you breathe into your heart, beloved one, feel the flavour of your soul, and see the most glorious colours. Each one brings an orb of light and a certain feeling, a certain experience, a certain journey. Each contains a certain life of its own. Within that orb of light are the people, the places, the giving and receiving of energy. So, follow one of those threads of light, dear one."

A rich colour attracts me. "This one feels like Tim."

"Yes. What do you feel, dear one?"

"I feel his love and strength. Oh, now he's reminding me I don't need to vocalise this. Our communication is telepathic. He says we are weaving our energies together."

A thought pops into my head. While waiting my turn to see Almora, for the first time when looking upon an artist's impression of him, I detected a physical resemblance to Tim. Intrigue gets the better of me. "By the way, Almora, do you and Tim have a close connection? Today I noticed a likeness between you and him."

"Yes, at times we do. Your observation holds a message for you, dear one. What are you aware of?"

"That he's to be found wherever I put my attention. He's going to be part of that focus because he is now a part of everything."

"Yes, indeed! And what do you notice has happened to his energy now, dear one? From this healing journey he's been on, and you've also been on?"

"Last night I recognised his energy, but I saw a distinct glow of rich magenta. Such a majestic, intense, rich colour. And his presence felt huge. So, he has matured and expanded?"

"Indeed, dear one!"

"My blessings to you, darling Tim. I honour your healing journey and your growth." Overwhelmed by his powerful presence and lost for words, I weep.

"Take a moment, beloved, just breathe. Feel that love wrapped around you."

The sense of being raised up by a thousand unseen hands returns for the first time since Tim's funeral. Otherworldly love that I had guessed might be angels surrounding me. Again, I sense the wafting and warping of blissful energies weaving a cocoon that embraces the interconnectedness of heaven on earth. Here, I straddle worlds. Reluctant to draw myself away, I hear Almora's polite "ahem."

"I can draw on these exquisite energies at any time?"

"Of course! At any time."

"And Tim's become omnipresent?"

"Indeed. It is a beautiful gift."

"Does he have a spirit name now?"

"Yes indeed. In your language, his vibrational harmonics would sound like 'Katoosh.' It means 'Eternal-Universal-Love.' Katoosh is a collective of souls. Therefore, your son no longer functions as an individuated soul."

We really do get more of him this way, I marvel. "Katoosh," I repeat, savouring the sound. "How wonderful." Something falls into place, and I ask, "Almora, Tim showed me a dream just after he passed. He shapeshifted into a white owl."

"What would you like to know, dear one?"

"Was that vision for now?"

"It was."

"You mean, eleven years ago, he appeared as my future guide, a white owl?"

"Yes, dear one. The owl sees all and says little, and also relates to the night energies. But you feel its presence and its wisdom. You have increased your understanding about telepathy and the diverse ways of communication."

"And now I just have to trust that communication."

"Yes, that communication and that wisdom."

Filled with inspiration, I ask Tim, "Is there anything you would like to add as we finish our beautiful book? A final message from you?"

Almora smiles. "Dear one, your son also has a request. He asks that you meditate with him later this day. He will give his answer then."

Almost choking with excitement, I arrive in Lyttelton with no memory of driving the last one and a half miles through the road tunnel. Instead, I feel as though I am travelling through a portal of expanded consciousness. Reaching the top of the steps at my house-sit, I fumble the key in the lock. Throwing my bag on the floor and patting Louie, a fluffy white Persian cat, I sit straight-backed in the middle of the leather couch. Tim arrives in an instant, his magenta mist swirling around the two-seater, turning Louie a delicate shade of lilac. I close my eyes and draw several long, deep breaths.

"Dearest mother, I greet you with the greatest love. Now that we both stand liberated from human limitations, our work together takes on a new meaning. Me in my realm, you in yours. An adventurous time lies ahead, but this time it is soul-directed, not driven by a desperate ego. My heart swells with joy when I peer into your future. There is much to look forward to. But for now, I am honoured to share these words for our first collaboration, our book.

"There is no ending, and that the relationship we have now, dear mother, extends beyond worlds, the universe, time and space. And from this place, I see more than ever and can bring help and support more than ever. But this freedom is not just for me and not just for you, dear mother. Through this book and through all of those you are meeting as a part of this journey is a great gift.

My life is not cut short.

And this is the message because for those who lose someone, especially a child, this loss is one of the greatest pains and beliefs they can have.

So, my message is:

"There are no endings.
I Am the Ever Being of Life."

EPILOGUE

*I*t's July 2024 and Laura spends a wintry week with me in the tiny village of Tokaanu. My geothermal haven sits at the southern edges of Lake Taupo in the heart of New Zealand's North Island. Spirit directed me here seven years ago, and now they say this chapter is complete. I don't know where my next base will be. I no longer take leaps of faith, my trust in my Higher Self now firmly established.

During Laura's stay, a copy of 'Portals' arrives in the letterbox. This book by international bestselling author, Freddy Silva, went straight to number one in four countries - and I'm delighted to be a contributing author. A portal is a location where humans can access nonphysical worlds with relative ease. My portal story describes a major energy activation in 2010 at Castle Hill/Kura Tawhiti, the heart chakra of New Zealand/Aotearoa. Twenty-four years ago, that activation heralded the start of my current work as a planetary activator. I believe nothing is by chance, and it occurred within weeks of my first pilgrimage to Glastonbury, the heart chakra of the world. You may recall reading about that in Chapter 16. I didn't have much of a clue what that meant at the time, and probably that was just as well.

Laura loves to celebrate success just as much as Tim and decided to toast the arrival of Portals. We didn't smoke a cigar, but instead donned our pyjamas in the middle of a wet afternoon, lit the fire, made dips for our chips, and poured pinot gris into the best crystal. We snuggled in to watch a Michael McIntyre show, an extremely funny English comedian and a keen observer of human nature. At the same time, our beloved friend, Raeul, happened to be reading over 'The Sound of a Broken Heart' in the next room. He told us later that tears streamed down his face while reading my heart-wrenching struggle to tell Laura her brother had died. Paradoxically, at the same moment he heard us howling hysterically with laughter in the next room, the joyous sound of healed hearts.

Tim's timeless wisdom of the silent white owl who sees much and says little is a constant presence. A featherlight touch of his wise wingtips corrects my course when needed, guides my angle of flight, and expands my perspective. This sweet, eternal relationship will continue to soar for the rest of my days on earth. I'm not by any means his only project. His area of interest is vast. At one stage he described collaborating with the archangels as their messenger and studying healing under the tutelage of Archangel Raphael. Recently he explained I'd feel his presence less while he focused on learning everything he could about music. Meantime, a different aspect of his soul reincarnated six years ago, and another plans to return with a focus on healing through music, combining those two fields of study. These aspects are not Tim, they are his soulmates, created from the same oversoul as Tim, but there will be recognisable traits and characteristics – for we have plans to meet again.

Unrolling the map of my sacred life, I see the paths I was destined to take lit up like a constellation of stars. Although, being human, I recognise some dalliances and distractions,

EPILOGUE

but there are no major deviations from my preordained soul agreements.

Magic is something humans love to flirt with. They romanticise otherworldly myths and legends, emotionally and intellectually, but keep it at a safe distance, firmly relegated to the world of fantasy and fiction. If I can shift this perspective, even a little, to open humanity to tangible magic in their everyday life, I will be content. Because when I look back over the twelve years since first publishing this book, I can only describe my life as one of pure, utter magic.

Aware of this role for several years now, I am one of the first wave messengers living through huge upheaval on the planet. For twelve years my work has been a living, organic thing which constantly shifts and changes. And it is filled with earth magic, not only as I make pilgrimages to sacred sites around the world as a conduit of Source energies, but in daily life.

Glastonbury stays hugely significant in my life and has already called me back another three times - by a different name now - neither Annette nor Corky, but as Annwyn, a name from a previous lifetime. In the Welsh tradition, Annwyn is the name of the Otherworld, the place first shown to me by Tim during the white owl dream a few days after his departure.

I began writing my second book with the intention of describing an extraordinary series of events following the Glastonbury pilgrimage and what everyday life looks like having surrendered to my Higher Self. But first, I needed to provide background of how I got to where I am now, including the pivotal recalled lifetime as the 16th century Glastonbury abbot. But the abbot had other ideas. Halfway through the book he made it quite clear he was not just an accessory like a cushion on an oak settle - he insisted on having a book all to himself!

How did he let me know? One sleepless night around 3am, I stood on an upper storey deck sipping cocoa and staring at the sky. I saw a falling star. I see those often and didn't pay much heed. Looking in another direction, I took another few sips of cocoa and saw something resembling the tail end of a gorgeous fireworks display - a falling trail of colourful sparks of light. I immediately thought of my book splitting into two. The next morning I awoke with the absolute clarity I was now writing two books. This is just one small example of the earth magic spontaneously occurring through the natural alignment with my Higher Self.

Hence, my forthcoming book is called *'The Light in the Abbey'* and the working title of the third book is *'Keys to Katoosh'*. And that could all change!

Under Tim's guidance, Spirit also utilises me as a planetary activator, but that is getting ahead of things. That story will be told in the third book. Each book demonstrates the incredible changes to my life after sucking every seed from the fruits of grief. At the end of the day before sleep I thank my beloved son in spirit, now known as *Katoosh*, for his enduring white owl wisdom. Katoosh means 'Eternal-Universal-Love' and is a soul collective. Thank you, darling Tim, for enabling me to know myself.

'To Know Thyself,' as Yeshua said,
is to know the highest version of ourselves.
Our authentic higher selves.

ANNWYN

After her teenage son died in 2000, New Zealander ANNWYN was guided by ascended masters for nearly twenty-five years, absorbing and integrating their timeless, universal wisdom into her daily life. From the realms of Spirit, Tim, now known as Katoosh, is one of her main teachers. She has inspired others with her practical perspective as a spiritual author, mentor, and energy healer, for fifteen years.

ANNWYN describes her life as one filled with enchantment-like magic. She adds that it's really quantum physics, understanding how to work with the energies of our universe. She says it's a natural consequence of surrendering to her Higher Self, and everyone can live this way if they wish.

Please subscribe to her website to find out about her books, events, and personal mentoring/healing sessions https://www.annwynvibe.com/

You can also connect with ANNWYN here https://www.facebook.com/AnnwynVibe

Other publications

ANNWYN is a contributing author to *Portals* by leading researcher of ancient civilisations and international bestselling author, Freddy Silva. *Portals* became a #1 bestseller in four countries within days of its release, signalling global intrigue with sacred sites where the laws of physics behave differently and physical and non-physical realities overlap.

Portals, by Freddy Silva, published by Sacred Stories Publishing, Fort Lauderdale, FL USA, 2004

Available here in various formats: https://invisibletemple.com/portals-book.html

Forthcoming publication

The Light in the Abbey, a story of holding the light during the dark decades of church reformation. Set during the 16th century Tudor time of King Henry VIII, a young boy, Richard Whiting, is destined to spend his life behind cloistered walls, eventually, and most reluctantly becoming the last abbot of England's iconic Glastonbury Abbey. A Celtic Christian at heart, the name taken by underground pagans, he must straddle the worlds of earth magic and late medieval Catholicism.

ACKNOWLEDGEMENTS

First and foremostly, I acknowledge my son, Tim. This is really his book.

"How can I grieve for a son who gifted me my authentic self

How can I mourn loss when I have found eternal truths

How can I regret a single action when it was all preordained

How can I feel pain in my heart when joy feels so much better

How can I be apart from him when there is no separation

How can I miss him when he's there the instant I call

How can I fail to see him when he is everywhere I place my attention

How can I not hear him when he is in the silence

How can I yearn for hugs when his love embraces me

How can I think I'm forgotten when he sends hawks and rainbows

How can I grieve death when there are no endings?"

Secondly and not any less, I honour my daughter, Laura. This is her book too. We experienced the same challenging event through different lenses, designed to evolve our respective areas of soul growth. Even though she looked at me at times and shook her head, asking, "Where has my mother gone?" she never held me back from the experiences that took me away from her. And despite this added layer of abandonment and grief, she allowed me the freedom that arises from unconditional love. Thanks to her, too, we learned the difference between human and soul suffering, and also how suicide is perceived from a spiritual perspective.

On that note, my heart-felt thanks go to the family of Floyd Walker who supported sharing Floyd's struggle in Chapter 19.

I have enormous gratitude for Raeul Pierard, my champion sounding board who endlessly discussed and read the revised edition in between buckets of coffee and barrels of laughter and, at times, tears. Also, for the encouragement from Karen Bowller, midwife to emerging inspired writers.

Lastly, I bow my head in awe at the support and guidance from all those in Spirit who have steered and shaped this interdimensional collaboration. A meeting of worlds, a meshing of ideas and a great opening of hearts.

www.ingramcontent.com/pod-product-compliance
Lightning Source LLC
Chambersburg PA
CBHW022043290426
44109CB00014B/963